HORSE HOUSEKEEPING

MARGARET AND MICHAEL KORDA

Horse Housekeeping

Everything You Need to Know
to Keep a Horse at Home

Collins

An Imprint of HarperCollins*Publishers*

HarperCollins books may be purchased for educational, business, or sales promotional use. For information, please write: Special Markets Department, HarperCollins Publishers, 10 East 53rd Street, New York, NY 10022.

FIRST EDITION

Illustrations by Michael Korda

Designed by Amy Hill

Library of Congress Cataloging-in-Publication Data is available upon request.

ISBN-10: 0-06-057308-2
ISBN-13: 978-0-06-057308-9

05   06   07   08   09   ❖ / RRD   10   9   8   7   6   5   4   3   2   1

For all the people who have been

part of our barn at Stonegate over the years,

and in memory of Harold Roe.

Contents

Foreword   *xi*

Introduction   *xiii*

CHAPTER ONE

A Horse at Home   *1*

CHAPTER TWO

Fencing and Paddocks   *27*

CHAPTER THREE

Halcyon Days   *45*

CHAPTER FOUR

The Barn Routine   *71*

CHAPTER FIVE

The Care of the Horse   *83*

CHAPTER SIX

Boarding   *95*

CHAPTER SEVEN

People　*99*

CHAPTER EIGHT

Feeding and Caring for the Horse　*117*

CHAPTER NINE

Tack　*141*

CHAPTER TEN

Horse Clothing　*149*

CHAPTER ELEVEN

Equipment　*155*

CHAPTER TWELVE

Care for the Aging Horse　*163*

CHAPTER THIRTEEN

Winter Weather, and How to Deal with It　*169*

CHAPTER FOURTEEN

A Day in the Life　*177*

Acknowledgments　191
Resources　193
Sample Expense Budget　195
Index　199

FOREWORD

We both were thrilled to see *Horse Housekeeping*. This great read is a powerful and practical reference for the horse owner who dreams of having her own horse, in her own backyard, and who wants to get it right from day one. We both had the luxury of having our first horses at our respective homes. Having a practical reference like this would have saved our parents tons of angst and stress about the responsibilities associated with having a horse at our own property. (While David's mother, Sally O'Connor, grew up with horses, Karen's parents, Phil and Joanne Lende, and David's father, Jay, learned the hard way!)

This book is a must-read for every horse owner, as Michael and Margaret Korda go into great depth on good, solid care of our wonderful friend, the horse.

Karen and David O'Connor
The Plains, Virginia
June 2005

INTRODUCTION

By Margaret Korda

When Michael first said to me that his publishers were interested in a book about keeping "backyard horses," and thought it was a project we could do together, I immediately said I could not do that. We did not have a "backyard" operation here, and I could only write about what I knew firsthand. Then I thought about why I had said that—and so quickly too. I came to the conclusion that it was because I associated the word "backyard," with something tacky, rundown, perhaps shoddy and poorly operated. I found that not to be so. According to *Merriam-Webster's 11th Collegiate Dictionary*, the definition of the adjective "backyard" is "lacking professional training: amateur." And has been in use in that sense since 1740.

I can only write about how our barn is run and our horses are cared for; I cannot speak for others. I have no experience of keeping horses in other parts of the United States than where we live, in the Northeast. Many readers may say, "My God, I would never do that," or "That's all well and good for them, but . . ." I do not know many people today who have their own barn. Most riders I know keep their horse(s) in boarding stables, for many reasons. And those reasons should be very carefully explored before deciding to keep your horses at home. A few of them might be that you will not have to be faced 24/7 with the everyday barn problems, such as turn-out, grooming, mucking stalls, calling the vet when necessary, taking care of the worming and shots, or making the farrier appointments, ordering the feed and bedding, dealing with a fresh foot of snow on the five foot drifts, or slogging back and forth through six inches of mud in the spring. And there will more than likely be the use of an indoor ring—most important in the Northeast winter—as well as trails, and, if you are lucky, someone to exercise your horse(s) if you are not able to ride. Trainers are on hand, should you be interested. These are just a few things to think about. And believe me it will be expensive!

Not, of course, that running your own barn will be any less costly; it won't. But if you are like me, then all the headaches and heartaches that come along with having your horses at home, the pleasure and the rewards, far outweigh keeping them elsewhere. All the same, even if you are lucky enough to have great help, having your horse(s) at home doesn't mean you can drive out the gates on a whim—I have the best of help, but it still takes months of planning to go on vacation!

Anyway, here is our experience, so read on.

HORSE HOUSEKEEPING

CHAPTER ONE

A Horse at Home

Not so very long ago, keeping a horse at home was a natural thing to do, like keeping a car today.

Even in the great cities, the horse was omnipresent and essential. In London's fashionable West End, the mews—where tiny houses and apartments now sell for a fortune—were merely cobbled alleyways behind the great houses, where the family's horse (or horses) were kept, and above whose stable the coachman and the groom were lodged. Until the invention of the motor car, the horse was as much part of the urban scene as it was of the rural—horse manure was an unavoidable presence too, of course, and the crossing sweeper at each corner of the better neighborhoods held his hand out for a tip, in return for which he swept a narrow path clean of manure so that ladies, delicately raising their long, full skirts a few inches, could cross the street without soiling their shoes or the hem of their skirt. Gentlemen wore spats to guard their ankles against splashes of horse manure or horse piss, and streets were kept sanded or covered with dirt to give the horses safer footing than the bare paving stones, which of course produced a layer of filthy, malodorous mud whenever it rained.

Everywhere one traveled, it was the same—in Paris, Vienna, or New York, the streets were filled with horses—pulling cabs, or carts, or trolleys, or carriages. All these horses were, of necessity, lodged close to the family or to the place of business that employed them, from the well-to-do family's modest pair of carriage horses to the many huge draft horses of the delivery companies and the breweries, their presence unmistakable, particularly in warm weather. The horse was no mystery, and its care was common knowledge, like that of looking after a car today.

In the country, of course, the horse was even more important. The horse pulled the plow, the harrow, the hay cart—without healthy horses a farmer would have been unable to plant and harvest his crops, or to deliver them to the nearest market town or railway terminus. Even the most ignorant of farmers knew the basics of how to look after a horse, and even the cruelest and most hard-hearted of them would make sure his horses were fed and cared for, even if his workers, or indeed his own children, were going hungry. The horse, after all, was a working animal, a valuable investment, as well as a means of transport. You needed to be able to recognize "Monday Morning Disease" (when a horse "tied up" from not being worked over the weekend), or how to deal with a colic, or how to get a horse back on its feet if it got "cast" in its stall. The farmer depended on the horses' health and soundness, exactly the way he now depends on his car, pickup truck, or tractor to start up at the turn of the key. The knowledge of how to care for horses went from commonplace and normal to rare and esoteric in one generation. In the Western world, the generation that preceded the First World War was raised in the Age of the Horse; the generation that followed was raised in the Age of the Automobile. Those born in the former knew how to replace a lost shoe, adjust a bit or a piece of harness; their sons learned how to repair a flat tire, clean a carburetor, or change a spark plug instead. "Horse sense" was no longer passed down from generation to generation, but became the province of special groups, those which centered around the race track, the show ring, or fox hunters, in any case people for whom riding was a sport or a recreation. Looking after horses was poorly paid, hard work, and a peripheral skill in the Machine Age, increasingly irrelevant as humans took to the road in cars, or to the skies in airplanes, and as the internal combustion engine replaced the horse on farms.

In fact, the horses themselves could now be vanned to polo matches and fox hunts, or even flown from one country to another for racing, grand prix jumping, eventing, international driving and endurance competition, the Olympics, etc.—in short, even among those who still clung to the horse for one reason or another, the stable and manure pile were no longer close to the home, where they had once unmistakably been.

As the knowledge of how to look after horses waned, the idea of keeping a horse (or horses) *at home* increasingly came to seem like a difficult and challenging undertaking—eccentric, demanding, fraught with problems. Yet, no more than ninety years ago (a mere blink in the ten thousand-year-old relationship between man and horse), nobody thought twice about it; the horse was part of everyday life, caring for it as unremarkable as looking after a cat or a dog.

Of course this is true of a lot of other things—we buy our milk in cartons at the supermarket now, rather than learning how to milk a cow, let alone how to look after her—and inevitably each scientific or technological advance produces a whole body of knowledge, once considered vital, which we can promptly forget. Automobile engines are now largely computer controlled and are designed to be tinker-proof, the "shade tree mechanic" having been replaced by a technician in a white coat with a hand-held computer terminal. Many of the skills which once, not so very long ago, seemed essential are now of limited use and importance, looking after horses among them.

Still, if what you want is to keep horses at home, you should take heart from the fact that it was a natural thing to do until quite recently. Today, of course, the horses are more likely to be kept as a hobby than out of necessity, but that changes nothing—the same needs, rules, and precautions still apply; the basics haven't changed any more than the horse itself has.

The idea of keeping horses at home is bound to seem like a challenging one if you've never done it before, as is often the case with people who take up riding these days, and it is undeniably time-consuming. But it *can* be done—we did it, after all, starting over twenty-three years ago on a farm with twenty acres of land (our acreage has since increased), just ninety miles up the Hudson River from New York City, and this book is the product of that experience.

It goes without saying that differences in climate and geography have to be taken into account. There are obvious differences between keeping horses in the West and in the Northeast, or keeping them in places where there is a real winter (as we write this it is below zero outside, and snow lies thick on the ground, with more in store) as opposed to places like Florida, where you're not likely to wake up in the morning and find the water in the horses' buckets frozen solid, or two feet of snow covering your fields. Still, horses have survived pretty well everywhere that man has taken them, and the basics for keeping them alive and well haven't changed much either.

A word about ourselves is perhaps in order at this point. Margaret was born in the country, grew up on a farm in England, started riding at the age of three, and gave up a career as a model in order to have a barn at home, with her own horses in it, and eventually to compete successfully in the Northeast. Horses, you might say, are in her blood. Michael is a city boy, whose horses had always been boarded in commercial stables and who came to keeping horses at home late in life, and with a certain amount of initial reluctance and skepticism. Despite writing *Horse People,* he does not pretend to possess any expertise on the subject of keeping horses, beyond writing out checks and trying to look wise, or at any rate, calm. We have a barn in the country—in an area that is becoming, alas, ever more swiftly developed and suburbanized—in which we currently keep five horses. As we write this, two of our horses are old and semi-retired, one is an aging eventer, now mostly ridden by Michael, and two are in different stages of training as Margaret's competition horses. Margaret essentially runs the barn, and knows a lot more about horses than Michael does, so when you hear the voice of wisdom and authority here, it's apt to be Margaret's.

In general Margaret supervises everything in the barn, which usually amounts to a full day's work, though she tries to be out of her riding clothes and into the bath at some point in the day, as opposed to being one of those barn ladies who is still wearing riding breeches and has straw in her hair at dinner time, or beyond.

She recalls how it all began: "When we first saw the property, on a gloomy March day in the pouring rain, I had a broken leg from a riding accident and was on crutches. So of the original nineteen acres most of what I could see was just around the house and the views of the lawns stretching into woods. I did, of course, see the barn, though I do not remember going inside that first time, and I did notice a small fenced field behind the barn, with of all things, an above-ground swimming pool.

"*That will have to go,* was my first thought. Apart from the one field and another unfenced cleared area, everything else I could see through the rain was overgrown with weeds and covered with rocks, not to mention dozens and dozens of unwanted cedars. *By June,* I thought, *this will be a jungle, waist high. If we want to do something with this, we will have to move fast!* We were in the house by the beginning of May, with no furniture other than a few odds and ends. Our two horses did not arrive until September, so we had some time to prepare for them. By then, we already had somebody to run the barn: Roxanne Bacon. Her husband, Richard, would look after the house and barn when it came to electricity and plumbing, and a tough and resourceful old man named Harold Roe would do outdoor work.

Getting the barn in shape took up much of Richard and Roxie's time. Harold removed the offending pool, fixed the fencing in the one existing field, and put in new gates. A large effort was made by us, and any guests who showed up that first summer—for what I imagine they must have thought would be a great change from going out to the Hamptons, but with all the same creature comforts—to pick up the rocks in the other cleared area. Some guests gamely pitched in, apparently under the impression this was something one normally did in the country while visiting for a weekend. Others appeared bewildered, immediately left to go antique shopping, and never came back to visit us again.

Building a barn from scratch is in some ways an easier proposition than renovating and restoring an existing structure, particularly since many new barns now come in pre-designed sections, which just have to be sunk into a concrete foundation in the right order. What's more, with a new structure there's ample scope for building in all those things you've always wanted, whatever they may be—a washing bay, or a hay chute, or a comfortable toilet for the help (or yourself).

When you modify an existing structure, especially an old one, there's less opportunity to custom-make it to resemble the barn of your dreams. Old barns have their charms—including wonderful old weathered beams that people will pay a lot of money for these days, in case you take the opposite approach and decide to tear the whole thing down—but given the decline in family farming throughout most of the country, most of them are in poor shape, suffering from decades of neglect. With an old barn, most of the money will go to fix what's about to collapse, rather than to transform it into something completely different.

We took a certain minimalist approach, both because of money—we had cracked open our nest egg to buy the house— and because it seemed to both of us more sensible to take the project step by step.

Margaret remembers the transformation in detail.

"The basic building as it was when we first saw it, is the same today. Three eleven-by-eleven-foot stalls on either side of the aisle, dutch doors on the outer sides, and hinged half doors on the inside. Double hinged doors at the north end opening outward, and at the opposite end, but facing east, a second set of sliding double doors. Across the aisle from them, an area which was the feed room and on the south end, the tack room.

"I say the basic building, for even before we could move horses in, a lot of work had to be done. Richard Bacon built a solid wall between one stall and the feed room, and added a door, so it could be closed up. The original tin-lined, large feed bin with its four divisions was there, and still is. Made locally, signed and dated. The area that would become our tack room was completely done over, again by Richard, with Roxie making sure certain things were in certain places, where she wanted them! The stalls had dirt floors, with wooden partitions between them, with sheep wire from about five feet up, to the ceiling. The windows were also covered with sheep wire. The aisle was concrete, over which we soon added a layer of blacktop. We didn't use sealant, which makes the surface slippery. It's worn very well over the years.

"There was an old hydrant on one side of the aisle, which we used for quite some time, but eventually replaced with an identical new one. Every square inch was covered in dirt and cobwebs. The hay loft, or "mall" as it is often called here, appeared not to have had much attention for many years. There was no lighting and little ventilation, a door at either end, a small one with a window on each side, and on the south end, a larger one, through which came deliveries—hay and straw. Starting in the loft you could see chinks of daylight—a sure sign that the roof was questionable.

"The bottom half of the interior—feed room, stalls, and aisle— was painted dark barn red, and the upper half had perhaps once been a 'light' color but when we first saw it, was definitely murky.

The electrical work badly needed upgrading. In fact every square inch needed attention.

"And so it began—Richard and Roxie worked day and night getting it all in order, so we could bring the horses home. Work was done on the electrical wiring. A ramp built for easier exiting out of the north doors, and covered with outdoor carpeting, to give traction. The inside of the barn was given a fresh coat of paint. Clay was brought in to freshen up and even out the stall floors, brackets with rings were fastened in two of the stall corners, from which water buckets would hang, with a stout wooden shelf for them to sit on, an added precaution to make them as secure as possible. Feed tubs were hung up in the third corner of each stall. Three pairs of heavy rings went up in the aisle for cross ties, and lead ropes soon appeared attached to them. Blanket racks were put up outside the two stalls we would be using, as were hooks for the halters, and of course, eventually, there would be nameplates on the stall doors as well. A shelf was put up for Roxie's radio, and wall fixtures were installed to hang our barn cleaning equipment on. Smaller hooks for hoof-picks and other small tools, and a grooming box with assorted brushes and grooming necessities appeared in readiness. The feed room was addressed, the floor was painted—a mistake we quickly discovered, since it was too slippery—then covered with inexpensive outdoor carpeting (it's still there twenty-five years later!), a trestle table was positioned along the length of one wall and, of course, the inevitable hooks and brackets put up on the walls.

"Feed buckets were purchased along with a measuring scoop, rubber water buckets for the stalls, and a metal water trough for our one and only paddock, for the first fall and winter. We quickly learned to buy a heating coil! The purchases continued: salt blocks and holders, wheelbarrow, and basic shovel, pitch forks, rake, muck bucket, later to come with its own cart.

"In the tack room, Richard put rough oak boards on the floor—they are there today—and lined the walls with wood. There were windows on three sides, long glued shut with coats of paint. Below the ones overlooking the lawn, he built a 'window seat,' where we put a fitted pad covered with an appropriately darkish material, so the dirt would not show too quickly. He put up a dropped ceiling with insulation, and fluorescent strip lights. A propane gas heater was installed, as well as saddle racks and bridle brackets, our two tack trunks, and a built-in medicine cabinet with glass doors, containing the very basic things we would need for starting out. Across the room from a chest-high counter top, under which were two good size shelved cupboards, Richard put up more shelves, and under them a clothes rack, all very useful and still with us. But the *pièce de résistance* was his padded saddle rack, for cleaning saddles and setting out the tack in readiness for use. He built in more shelves below, and hung a four-pronged tack hook, for cleaning bridles, from the ceiling above it. Feed and bedding were ordered; we were ready to go!

"Well, *getting* there, anyway.

"Has it changed in twenty-four years? The answer is: yes and no."

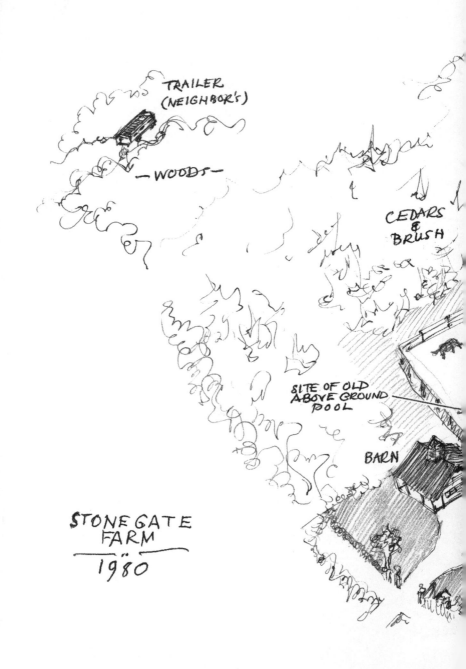

TRAILER
(NEIGHBOR'S)

—WOODS—

CEDARS
&
BRUSH

SITE OF OLD
ABOVE GROUND
POOL

BARN

STONE GATE
FARM

1980

Margaret recalls that one of the major jobs we did as soon as we could was to replace the old electrical wiring, bringing it strictly "up to code," adding to the aisle lights, and installing overhead lights in the stalls, and in the hay loft, with the bulbs inside the metal brackets, an important safety precaution, so in the event of a light fixture being hit, you might get a bump, or even an injury, but no broken glass. And at the same time we had smoke detectors installed overhead in each stall and a fire alarm system put in the tack room.

The stall floors are covered with rubber mats now, and the sheep wire was replaced many years ago with bars, both between

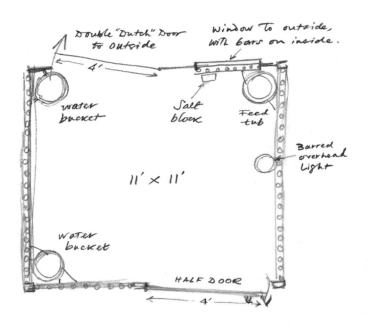

FLOOR PLAN OF A TYPICAL STALL

the stalls and covering the windows, and the latter can now be opened for cleaning. We had a trap door cut into the ceiling of the 'hay' stall, so we can drop hay down into a stall, not into the aisle—much easier for cleaning up. All the tops of the half doors and any exposed edges/corners have had metal channel put on, and I recommend doing so, since it stops damage to those areas, such as you get when you have a horse who likes to chew or crib, and cuts down on splinters as the material ages!

Feed and water buckets have been replaced a few times. A new hydrant was put in within the last year. Some boards have been replaced here and there, to the sides of stalls and the loft floor.

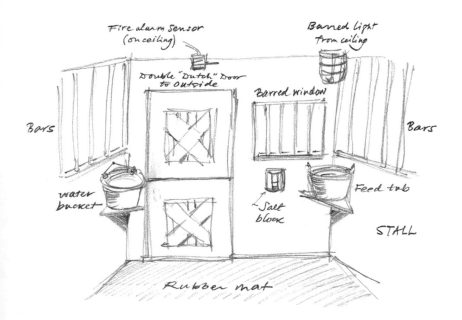

TYPICAL STALL

DOORS ON THE
OUTSIDE ARE
"DUTCH" i.e.
DOUBLE DOORS

STONE PO[...]
OVERHANG

WINDOW

WINDOW

MEDICINE
CABINET

WINDOW
SEAT

CLOSET

A/C

FEED
BIN

MIXING
TABLE

FEED
TUB

SADDLE
RACKS

WATER
BUCKETS

WINDOW

GAS
HEATER

TACK
TRUNK

FEED
BIN

SADDLE
RACKS

WINDOW

FEED
BIN

BARS

AISLE

SADDLE CLEANING
RACK

NOTICE BOARD

FIRE EXTINGUISHER

BARS

COUNTERTOP
STORAGE
BENEATH

CLOSET

WATER
BUCKETS

WINDOWS

SLIDING DOORS

FEED
TUB

TELEPHONE

WINDOW

OVERHANG

FLAGSTONES

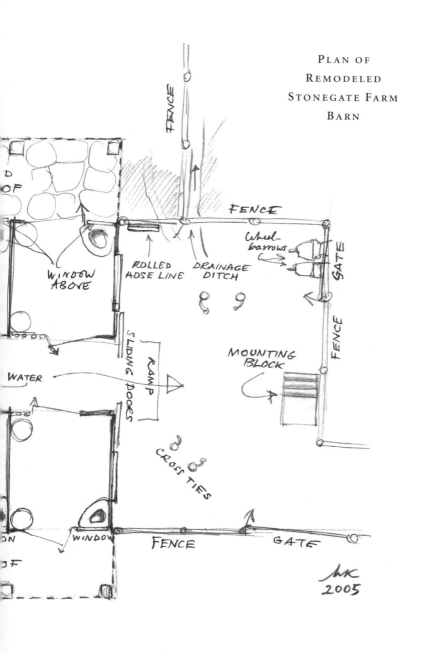

PLAN OF
REMODELED
STONEGATE FARM
BARN

FENCE

FENCE

D
OF

WINDOW
ABOVE

ROLLED
ADSE LINE

DRAINAGE
DITCH

Wheel-
barrows

FENCE GATE

SLIDING DOORS

RAMP

MOUNTING
BLOCK

WATER

CROSS TIES

ON

OF

WINDOW

FENCE

GATE

hK
2005

There have been several new coats of paint, but we still keep the bottom half 'barn red' and the top half white. Nameplates have come and gone. (The old ones are kept on a wall in Michael's office.) In addition to the individual blanket racks outside each stall, we have added two multi-railed hanging racks in the aisle, for use in the winter for all turn-out blankets, rain sheets, stable blankets/sheets, etc. We take these down during the summer, since then they become just dust collectors.

Electric fans now go up each summer, attached to the outside of each stall. We have two milk crates hanging on a wall angled off the aisle, in which we keep polo wraps, galloping boots, and bell boots, and Star's donut (a soft rubber ring which fits above his nearside hind hoof, to stop him from "clipping" himself). They are always covered with a towel, to keep the dust off, and it is easy to throw into the washing machine once a week. And, except in wintertime, outside the barn, by the cross ties, I have two similar crates hanging from a fence rail, with assorted sponges, a couple of brushes, a "jelly" mitt (for grooming), sweat scraper, shedding blade, a hoof pick, and the hose nozzle when not in use. A rolled hose hangs on a reel next to the crates most of the year. (It's useful to roll up your hose nozzle end first, by the way, that way the end you attach to your outlet is immediately at hand.) The ramp leading out of the north end of the barn has been replaced several times, as has the outdoor carpeting, but the original mounting block is still there, twenty-four years later!

The feed room is virtually the same. The only change being the "feed list," kept on a dry-erase board, from time to time. And every few years we get a new small vacuum for the tack room and feed room. The tack room had the ceiling and lighting fixture replaced recently, along with a new heater, though in fact we got the exact same model as the original. Richard's window seat is still there, but with a new cushion! And this last summer we treated ourselves to a small window air conditioner in the tack room.

Separating the barn from the house was the "studio barn," an even more decrepit structure which must have been converted from keeping livestock to a garage at the turn of the century, when it had received a concrete floor and big, swinging doors, which, when the wind caught them, were as hard to handle as the unreefed sails of a big schooner in a storm. The previous owners had, at some point, turned it into a summer art school for local children, in the easy-going days before the building codes and safety regulations would have required an almost total rebuild for that purpose, but it showed no signs of ever having been used for horses in modern times. At one end there was a sink and a stove, along with many abandoned art projects, but it was clear enough that the best we could hope for when it came to this building was turning it back into a garage. Two other "outbuildings" testified to the property's more rural past, a chicken house and a shed at the bottom of the lawn that might have served for anything, except perhaps keeping horses in.

A few years after we moved the horses into the barn, we had

the adjacent building, the "studio barn," in which we garaged the cars, razed and rebuilt, as it was coming apart at the seams. Our friend and local builder, Detlef Juress, did this work for us, and in the rebuilding he put in a separate laundry room/toilet. This was a godsend, as until this time, any hot water had to come from the house, and anyone needing a bathroom, also had to trek into the house. Now we have the luxury of a washer/dryer, large sink with hot/cold water, refrigerator, and toilet only a few steps from the tack room.

Once you have these things at hand, you wonder how on earth you ever managed before—every time the tack was cleaned, over to the house you went, with a bucket to get hot water; if a horse had an abscess, back and forth for hot water to soak his foot in; if a wound needed hot packing, the same thing. Every piece of horse laundry was done in our washing machine in the kitchen, not a great idea! But then, as Margaret reminds herself from time to time, she lived in Kenya for two years without any form of refrigeration, thought nothing of driving 180 miles round trip to see a movie in Nairobi, and had not even heard of air conditioning.

It's easy to obsess about barns—and many do—but the major reason for having a barn is, simply, that it provides protection for the horses from extreme weather conditions. Another, less obvious reason, may be that a well-designed barn keeps dirty boots, tack that needs cleaning, hay, straw, shavings, manure, etc., out of the house. A good rule is to keep everything that has to do with the horses outside the house as much as possible, including those boots that you wear when you're mucking stalls, or the saddle pads that need washing, or the old rain gear that smells to high heaven. If both members of a family are keen "horse people," it's probably alright for the stable to intrude upon the house, up to a point. But in families where only one person (or one person plus a certain number of children) is a horse person, the tack drying in the bathroom, the saddle pads filling the washing machine with horse hair, and the muddy, manure-scented boots in the hall, may not be a good idea. Even the least house proud and fastidious of men will probably not enjoy having to move a couple of dirty bridles and girths to one side in order to bend over the bathroom sink to shave, or appreciate buckets of bran in the kitchen sink. Even horse people like ourselves have been in houses where the horse seems to have taken over the home, and we didn't enjoy the experience for a moment.

We learned the hard way, partly because there wasn't a book like this available, and partly because of the feeling that we—more particularly Margaret—knew enough to plunge right in. We were helped by the fact that we were starting with a farm of sorts, or part of one. Admittedly, it hadn't been *worked* as a farm for several decades, and when it last was, sheep were kept here, rather than horses. The original farm, still known locally as "the old Hewlett farm," had been a dairy farm, then it got split up. The piece we bought, with the house and small barn on it (now known, by younger folk as "the old Hubner house") had tempted the Hubners into keeping sheep for a while, despite the fact that Mr. Hubner commuted into New York City five days a week, which meant that he had to be up hours before dawn and didn't get home until late in the evening, with the sheep to look after at the end of a full day in the office and several hours on the train.

Horses are not sheep of course, so it should have come as no surprise that putting up fences—and preparing our land for horse keeping—was almost as hard as renovating the barn, and certainly more expensive.

Needless to say, we took it for granted that our own horses would have plenty of space to move about in—after all, when we bought our house it came with twenty acres. Of course how much of the acreage was suitable for horses was another matter, as was preparing the ground and fencing it. Much of the rest of our land, that part of it which was flat and not covered by second-growth woods at any rate, had once consisted of cleared fields, and occasional traces of the time when this had been a dairy farm could still be found rusting away in the weeds. Turning this part of the property into handsome, fenced paddocks seemed like a minor task.

This was, of course, to reckon without Mother Nature, and the natural operation of "Murphy's Law." In our part of the country, even the most beautiful grassy lawn is barely covering layers of rocks which go down as deep as you can dig, or, worse yet, a shelf of solid rock which requires blasting to penetrate (as many people trying to build a swimming pool on their property have discovered at great cost).

There were other things we had overlooked: wet, boggy areas, where underground streams surfaced, areas where a shelf of solid rock peeked through the soil, limitless quantities of poison ivy, and endless bits of sharp metal and strands of rusty barbed wire, each piece guaranteed to puncture a horse's hoof. Eventually, Richard would be obliged to rent a metal detector, and go over the fields like somebody searching for landmines, harvesting an amazing number of sharpened metal stakes, pieces of corrugated iron, broken blades of every description, broken farm equipment dating back to the nineteenth century, and all the detritus you might expect from a hundred years or more of not particularly efficient or fastidious farming. (Apart from one or two old coins or buttons, nothing of even the mildest historical interest surfaced.)

We mention this because it's easy enough on a bright spring day to look out from your porch at a green field and tell yourself that it will make a terrific pasture for your horse once you've fenced it, but looking at it from a distance is very different from looking at it close-up. Those green, rolling fields you see in photographs of Kentucky Blue Grass horse farms are beautiful pastures for good reasons—over the past couple of centuries people have labored mightily to pull out the tree stumps, to drain the fields, to seed, fertilize, and lime the grass, and to make sure there's not a rock or a sharp object anywhere.

This is not, by any means, necessarily the case everywhere. First of all, some parts of the country are rough, rocky, sandy, and scrubby to begin with, but even where the potential for good pasture exists, it may take some work and planning to make it suitable for horses. You want to look at your property with a critical eye, and if necessary, seek the help of somebody who has some experience in judging these things, and knows something about livestock. A field that looks great on a nice summer day, may turn into a sodden quagmire in the autumn and the early

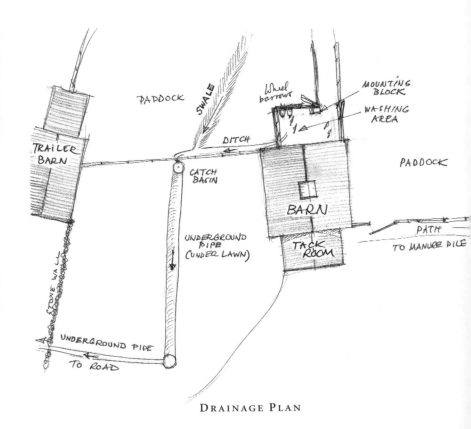

DRAINAGE PLAN

spring, producing mud that will pull the shoes right off your horse's feet. Good pasture for horses needs proper drainage, and if it doesn't have it, then it will have to be created, by somebody who knows what he's doing.

Even with the help of Harold Roe, who appeared in our lives before we had even bought the house to "look after things," and who felt for backhoes, bulldozers, swales, and ditches the kind of passion that some people feel for art or music or gourmet food, we still didn't manage to get everything 100 percent right—you can only do so much to alter the terrain you've got, unless you bring the Army Corps of Engineers in—and at a later date we had to build (and add to) an ever larger and more complicated drainage system.

Still, to give Harold his due, he usually knew what he was doing, and could at least be counted on to point out to us, that in his experience, water generally runs downhill, which is more than seems to have occurred to a lot of our neighbors when they moved from the city and began to keep horses.

The broader problems of horse keeping were not high on our agenda when we had first looked over our land and casually decided to remove the above-ground swimming pool which was such a blot on the landscape. Once it was gone—and once we had rented a backhoe to get rid of the unwanted cedars, and had Harold run his bush-hog over the area a couple of times—we sought Harold's advice about fencing.

Harold's answer to most questions was that he could do it himself, but on the subject of fencing for horses, he was more cautious. Post and rail fencing he could do, but the newer, fancier fencing needed a professional, and he had just the man to do it: Eddie McDonald, a part-time boiler maker and pig *aficionado* who specialized in putting up fencing for horse farms, and lived only a couple of miles away.

This, at the time, was a remunerative profession, since New York State had recently rewritten its tax code to promote Thoroughbred breeding, and dairy farms all over our part of the Hudson Valley were being hastily converted into horse farms by wealthy people whose accountants had told them they could write the whole thing off and save a bundle in taxes. And so they did, for a while. Then the law changed, and now many of these farms are derelict.

CHAPTER TWO

Fencing and Paddocks

Fencing, like so many things in the horse world, is at once regional and subject to changes in fashion. To some degree, fencing is determined by what's available in your part of the country. In our part of the country, where locust trees grow in abundance, locust rails are easy to come by, and post and rail fencing is put up in pretty much the same way that it was in the eighteenth century, though most people speed the process up with a mechanical posthole digger these days.

Over the years, maintaining the fencing has become a kind of preoccupation. You just can't check too often for weakening posts, broken rails, loose pieces of wire, tree limbs down on the fence line, worn out batteries on the electric fencing, or hornets' nests in unexpected places. Storms take their toll, of course, but in general, things just happen, and very often the people whose job it is to notice them walk right past without seeing a thing. Our friend Larry McMurtry, the Pulitzer Prize–winning author of *Lonesome Dove* (our favorite book and television miniseries), was raised as a cowboy on his father's cattle ranch near Archer City, Texas, and once, when he was asked what the most important thing in a cowboy's life was—the questioner was probably expecting a few words in praise of horses, or at least cows—he said, "Looking after fences."

Of course he was right. What cowboys do, most of the day, is ride out along the fence line and repair it. Even in the days when they still carried six guns, the tool that mattered to them most was a pair of good, strong pliers, with a notch for cutting wire, that, and of course a pair of stout work gloves. A break in the fence meant your cattle might be all over the range, mixed up with other people's, or lost, or stolen, so you kept your eyes on that all-important fence line, however long it was.

Once you've put in your paddocks or fenced in your fields, the security of your fence line had better be something you're sure of, that is if you don't want to be one of those unfortunate people running down the road from house to house in the middle of the night with a flashlight because your horses have broken out of their field and are out there somewhere in the dark, possibly galloping across other people's land toward the nearest highway for a fatal encounter with a speeding eighteen-wheel semi or a teenager in a souped-up Mustang who won't see them until it's too late.

Margaret chronicles the process in our case, step by step. "I knew from the start that I would want several paddocks, as I do not like to turn horses out together, and I like to rotate, allowing pasture to rest. Others may disagree and prefer to turn out their horses in the same field(s), and may not have a lot of choice if they don't have the room. However, I would strongly advise to try and plan to be able to rotate from one turn-out area to another. In an ideal world it would be great to have a laneway between each paddock, but very few small barns can afford to lose that amount of space.

"Consider the width of the gates prior to putting them in. Think about what types of vehicles may need to access these areas. For example in paddock #11 here, we need a sixteen-foot gate at the end closest to the manure pile, and another at the opposite end, to enable us to get the manure truck in and out. Gates should always rest on a block when closed, or in time they will sag and wreck their hinges. We use a chain to keep each gate shut. One end is permanently fixed to the gate post, the other has a double ended snap that goes around the post and fastens to an eyebolt. Our paddocks are situated so that horses are either next to each other or certainly never out of sight of another.

"I find horses turned out together in the same area are likely to have more injuries, usually as a result of being kicked or bitten. In the wintertime, they are very rough on each other's blankets, and a horse that went out in a two to three hundred dollar blanket can come back in wearing tatters. Feeding can be another problem, especially if one or more of the horses is aggressive.

It would be nice if each horse ate its hay and grain in the same amount of time, but it is never that way: the one who eats the fastest usually pushes the slower one away from his feed, or attempts to, resulting in roughhousing. You never want to put an older horse in this situation, as it will be the one to fare the worst. I can always tell if a new horse has come from a herd environment by its aggressive behavior at feeding time. I always make sure my barn help puts a halter and lead rope on a horse that shows any sign of misbehaving when food is around, leads it into the run-in shed, puts the food in the feed tub, turns him around, and steps outside before taking the halter off. I have seen what can happen when an employee thinks it does not matter.

"The first winter here in 1980 we did have to turn Hustle and Missouri out during the day together, although we have always kept horses in separate paddocks. Before that first winter set in, we had hired Eddie McDonald to put up three more paddocks for us, but they were not in usable shape until the next spring. And they were followed by two more in the summer. They all had 'Secretariat fencing,' (woven wire attached to treated posts, with a board along the top), which was the fencing of the moment. Would I use it again? No. It held up well, but required continual maintenance, and I mean *continual*. (We have since switched to post and rail fencing.)

"So within a year, we had six paddocks and a fenced in area we called the Pig Field, where we did indeed keep three pigs for a few years. But to put in the additional three paddocks we had to clear away more brush, cedars, weeds, and rocks. You seed grass and help the soil along with fertilizers. Then sit back and have some patience. If you use paddocks too soon and do not give the new grass a good chance to take root and grow, and hopefully have some rain to help it along, you might as well save yourself the labor and cost.

"But you will have no control over the weather: a drought can turn your beautiful paddocks into dust bowls in a short time. In the case of a severe drought, you may be fortunate enough to be able to irrigate, but we have to rely on well water, and there is always that fear of the well going dry.

"We had a pause for a few years from putting in more paddocks, while we built an indoor ring—it wasn't that the ring took several years to build, but you have to have your priorities in order, and you can only afford to do so much at a time. In the late fall of 1985 with now five, and on one occasion, six horses here, we started to clear more land and put in six more paddocks, one being quite small. The paddocks were all set up in a vaguely rectangular shape with two large cleared areas, known as the 'near area' and the 'far area' in the center of them. For years we used to put our stadium jumps in one or the other. Later we used these areas as paddocks too.

"For at least the first fifteen or sixteen years as most people did, and many still do, we carried water to the tubs in the paddocks by hand, bucket after bucket, one of the disadvantages of putting in paddocks farther and farther from the barn. And in the winter the water froze, so we trooped out several times a day just to break the ice, so the horses could have access to water.

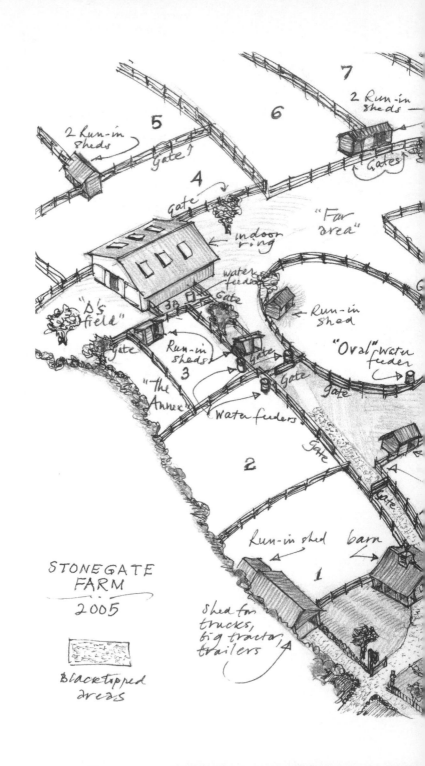

7

2 Run-in
sheds

6

5

2 Run-in
sheds

Gate

Gates

4

Gate

"Far
area"

indoor
ring

water
feeder

"D's
field"

3A

Gate

Run-in
shed

gate

Run-in
sheds

Gate

"Oval" water
feeder

3

"the
Annex"

Gate

Gate

Water feeders

Gate

2

Run-in shed

barn

STONEGATE
FARM
2005

1

shed for
trucks,
big tractor,
trailers

Blacktopped
areas

A

Trail to x-country
course and "powerline
Field"

Hardd's
bridge

TRAIL

Wappinger Creek

— Woods —

8

ter feders

← 2 Run-in-sheds

9

Gate

TRAIL

"ear
rea"

Gate

Gate

— Woods —

11

Manure
Pile

Run-in shed

acktop

"Pigfield"
Gate

gate

PATH TO MANURE PILE

Shed for tractor,
snow blowers, etc.

dry room

storage
shed

Garage

House

hl
2004

And when the horses came in at the end of the day, those tubs had to be emptied or by morning they would be solid ice and very tough to deal with. Never empty ice in the paddock, always make sure it is outside the fence, or you will have an ever grow- ing pile that, come warmer weather, will take weeks and weeks to thaw. About eight years ago, we had Detlef Juress put in an auto- matic watering system that services six of the winter paddocks. The other two are close to the barn and we have electric heating coils in large rubber tubs. The system is great, but you must learn how to take care of it and check it on a daily basis. And should you decide to invest in something such as this, you should know in advance, that when something goes wrong it can be a major headache, since all piping and electrical wiring is underground!

"Several years before the automatic watering system, we began building run-in sheds, starting with paddocks used in the wintertime, and gradually adding, as these sheds are as useful in summer as winter. They enable the horses to get into the shade, away from the bugs, and if they are smart enough, out of the rain. I also learned early on to have chicken wire put directly underneath the roof, otherwise you will find that families of pigeons will move in, and create a mess that you will constantly be dealing with. My run-ins are cleaned out everyday, and fresh bedding added when needed. We use those long handled dust mops to keep cobwebs at a minimum. It's a simple chore and worth the effort."

RUN-IN SHEDS

It is important to site your run-in sheds, if used all year round, or only for winter, facing south, and if you do not have this option, any direction but north. Our summer sheds face either east or south, as we did not have the choice in those paddocks to have the ideal site. And give thought to the size, always thinking larger if your budget allows, rather than smaller. Airy and light, rather than cramped and dark. A place your horse will want to go into, not be wary of entering.

"Our summer sheds have open fronts. In other words they are three sided, but ones used in winter (and if you use them all

TYPICAL RUN-IN SHED

year round) are three and a half sided, allowing extra protection for a horse during the winter weather. There is a feed tub with a salt block in a metal holder on the wall next to it. These tubs are attached to the shed wall in one of the corners, with double ended clips attached to three screw eyes, and can be taken down and cleaned when necessary, which is so much easier than having permanently attached feed tubs. The hay is put in the opposite corner, either on the ground or in a hay bag. If using hay bags, and especially if you are using a hay net, always make sure they are hung high enough; you do not want to have your horse pawing and getting a foot caught up. I keep the hay bag from swinging when the horse is eating by attaching it with double ended clips to screw eyes, one from which the bag hangs and the second two-thirds the way down the back of the bag. I use hay bags or nets in our sheds as I have found there is far less hay waste. When horses have sheds, they tend to go in and out of them all the time, so when flakes of hay are thrown on the ground, they more than often drag the hay out of the shed or get a good deal of it mixed in with the bedding.

"As most people have a water source in their turn-out area, there is no need to have additional water in the shed. But for those that don't, then two water buckets should be hung away from both feed tub and hay, with some heating device so that when the temperatures get low enough, your horse is guaranteed a supply of water that will not freeze. A thin layer of ice is acceptable as a horse can easily break this, but beyond that he needs help.

"I like to move horses from one paddock to another, so they do not get into the habit of always being turned out in one place, and you are not in the position of not being able to use one or another area for a certain horse. (Always check your paddocks regularly, especially after high winds or heavy rains, and if you have not used one for some time, before turning a horse out into them.) Switching horses back and forth between different paddocks does not always work out, and you learn quickly which ones cannot be next to each other, even with an electric fence between them. What often does work well is putting an older horse in a paddock between two younger horses who tend to get each other going if in neighboring paddocks. And when it's time to come in, always bring in the horses who run or start fooling around first. Don't ignore what they are doing—chances are you will either end up with a lost shoe, or an injury, and most certainly a badly torn-up field.

"In the fall, if you know, or are afraid, that deer hunters may come onto your property or close to your paddocks, even though your land is posted, use your turn-outs nearest to the barn. I never use the far paddocks during hunting season as they abut the land we bought soon after moving here, which has trails crisscrossing the rest of our property that tempt hunters and trespassers on four-wheelers. One fall, soon after we first came here and did not have many paddocks, we started taking the horses down to the "Powerline Field" (see map on pages 40–41). It had some old wire fencing, and Harold fixed up the gaps, and put in some slip rails to keep the horses in. It's very large and has great grass. The four horses we had at the time loved being down there for two or three hours a day, they didn't get into any trouble, as they were far too occupied eating, and in those days we had the time to take them down and bring them back later. We would ride one bareback and the others would follow.

"But one day during the bow-hunting season, Roxie went to bring them back to the barn, and Sundance had been shot in the fleshy part of the lower shoulder/upper leg. The arrow, which was not still in the wound had left a bloody mess. Roxie's cool-headedness in getting the horse back to the barn as quickly but as quietly as she could, then keeping cold running water on the wound until our vet, who at that time was Mike Murphy, arrived, I think was a major factor in the outcome. Mike sutured layer upon layer of torn tissue and then skin. A few months later you could hardly see a scar. But I never forgot it, and when we ride out today during the deer season, we have sleigh bells on our stirrups; I want the deer hunters, especially poachers, to *know* I am coming."

Our first paddocks had represented a sizeable investment in fencing, and it took a while before our bank account recovered enough to do more paddocks.

Considering the amount of time and trouble we took to remove rocks and roots and to have the fields sown with the right kind of grass, the sight of them in March or April, as the snow and ice melted away, revealing great clumps of slowly thawing horse manure and pools of thick mud, was enough to bring tears to our eyes, and still does so, every year. Yet somehow they manage to come back, and turn green again, despite periods of drought when they turn to brick-hard dust bowls, or periods of rain when they turn to gluey mud, with pools of water so deep that we have to use submersible pumps to prevent the barn from being flooded out.

Whatever our original intention had been, we added on fields as the mood took us, rather than hewing to some well thought out plan, with the result that some of the fields are more useful than others. A bird's eye view of the farm in its present configuration would therefore look like the drawing on the following pages.

Note that we have marked on the drawing of the farm today a few luxury items added over the years, the most obvious being an indoor riding ring, which, in our climate, is pretty much a necessity for keeping horses exercised through the winter.

As Margaret says, "I have inherited my father's love of the land. He knew more about land than I will ever know, the caring and maintenance of it. He knew it on a far, far larger scale than I will ever know, but it comes down to the same thing in the end. Whether you lease it or own it, remember it's only for a blink of time in the large picture. And it's 'needy.' You can spend twenty years caring for it—but forget it for six months, and you will have a multitude of problems. So whatever you call your turn-out areas—paddocks, fields, corrals, meadows, pastures—they will need taking care of. As will other area such as fields and trails.

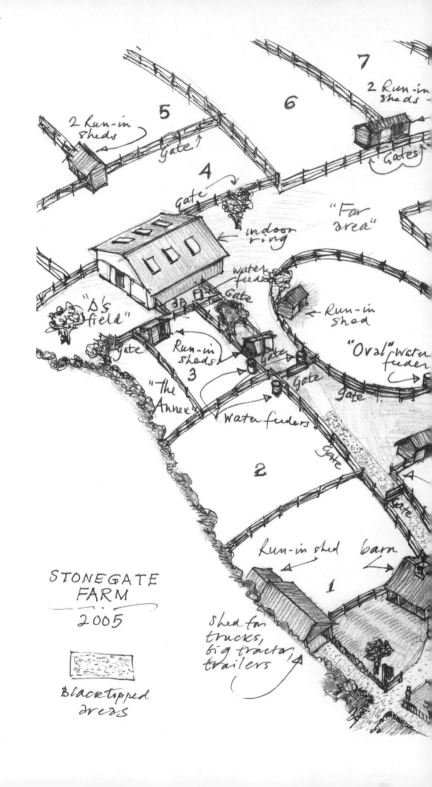

5

6

7

2 Run-in
sheds

2 Run-in
sheds

Gate

Gates

4

Gate

indoor
ring

"Far
area"

water
feeder

Gate

Run-in
shed

"D's
field"

"Oval" water
feeder

Gate

Run-in
sheds

Gate

Gate

3

Gate

"the
Annex"

Water feeders

Gate

2

Gate

Run-in shed

barn

STONEGATE
FARM
2005

1

Shed for
trucks,
big tractor,
trailers

Blacktopped
areas

A

Trail to x-country
course and "powerline
Field"

Hardd's
bridge

TRAIL

Wappinger Creek

— Woods —

TRAIL

8

water feeders

← 2 Run-in-sheds

Gate

9

— Woods —

"Near
area"

Gate

Gate

Manure
Pile

11

Run-in shed

"Pigfield"
Gate

Blacktop

gate

Gate

PATH TO MANURE PILE

Shed for tractor,
snow blowers, etc.

undry room

storage
shed

Garage

House

le
2004

"Everything depends so much on the weather. In '02 we mowed our 'Powerline Field' to get rid of the dry long winter grass on February 16th, but that's a rarity. Usually mowing in the fields begins in late April, and in the paddocks a week or two later. If the ground is dry enough I am on a tractor on the trails and fields no later than mid-to-late March. If you are using a 'finished' mower—a big one that is pulled behind the tractor—your chances of keeping pretty clean while mowing are good, but if you have a smaller 'midmount' mower, you had better be prepared to end up looking like something that most people would not want stepping into their barn, let alone their house, since you will be covered in grass cuttings. During dry periods, the dust is a problem, and on windy days, the cut grass will smother you once you hit the direction when the wind is not in your favor. But mowing is the best way to keep an eye on all your land; you see where the new holes are, where the frost has pushed up rocks during the winter, where the ground is still wet, how your fences are holding up, and what needs fixing.

"I personally like to mow the paddocks myself. And have Juan or Toby, who now work in the barn, as we write this, drag them, once or twice a week, weather permitting. This breaks up the manure. As often as we can, we use the weed-eater around the fence lines and gates, run-in sheds, and indoor ring. If the weeds are thick and tall, and the weather damp, they are raked up and thrown away immediately. If the weather is dry and sunny, we use the paddocks twenty-four hours after mowing; if not, we let two to three days go by before using. We are forced to let the back paddocks stay empty once the cold weather arrives, as they are fed water via a hose, which freezes. So usually by November the back paddocks are 'closed up': the shavings are raked up in the sheds, feed tubs get cleaned, and water tubs scrubbed and put away until spring. If we can time it right, and the weather cooperates, we lime the fields in the fall, but be sure to do this on a day with no wind! And watch the weather forecast, as it's best to have rain after doing this.

"We fertilize where needed, but do not seed; we are lucky that the grass always comes back in the spring! Check the fencelines during the winter, and remember to check your electric fence batteries, if you have them, the following spring. (We always date our batteries when we put them in—that way, as we learned over the years, we know when we should be getting new ones in stock.)

"Taking care of the fall leaves in your paddocks is another job for late October/early November. This chore is best done once you have had a couple of sunny days; dry leaves are easier to blow and carry. Nowadays I use my small tractor to blow them into a large pile, which is then forked onto a tarp, and moved to the nearby woods. But for many years, we raked and raked by hand, a back-breaking job. Trees are great for shade during the hot sunny days, and not much of a problem in large turn-out areas around the perimeters, but in small paddocks the fallen leaves can cover every square inch of ground.

"Where we are, Lyme disease has become epidemic, and the horses turned out in paddocks with a thick carpet of leaves, seem to come in with more ticks on them. Plus I don't like horses eating leaves, and some horses will eat anything! Any red maples we had when we started clearing for paddocks were removed, as their leaves are toxic to livestock."

What goes on with your horses *outside* the barn has to be planned for just as carefully as what goes on *in* the barn. Maybe more so.

CHAPTER THREE

Halcyon Days

When we first brought our two horses home, we had yet to make the full leap from living in the country on the weekends, to living there full time, and would not do so for several years. There were still whole areas of our twenty-acre property that we hadn't even thought much about, not to speak of the rooms in our house we had only entered once or twice, and hadn't even tried to furnish. It should not therefore be imagined that we turned our attention toward the stable only when the house itself was firmly established and running smoothly, and was our main residence. No such luck! On the contrary, we were still living in New York City and moving back and forth to the country every weekend, and when in the country drove every morning to where our horses were boarded to ride them.

Two great temptations were involved in the decision to move

the horses. The first was that our property, small as it was, was in those days connected to numerous "hunt trails," so it was clear that there was ample land to ride over, provided we asked our neighbors politely enough. There were, it seemed then, more places to ride than we could ever cover, in almost every direction (something that has changed over the years as "development" crept closer and closer, and houses replaced farms). The second was that, from the front door of the house, and indeed from many of its windows, the stable was simply sitting there, perhaps two hundred feet away at most, directly across the driveway. You could walk across to it in a few seconds, and you couldn't get out of your car without noticing it.

Had it been half a mile down the road, or more or less hidden from the eye, the idea of restoring it to some kind of useful function might not have taken root in our minds quite so easily. "Out of sight is out of mind," applies to buildings, as well as to other things. But the stable, whatever else you could say about it, was definitely not out of sight—every time you opened the front door there it was, at once a temptation and a challenge.

Of course, one argument in favor of rebuilding the stable and putting our two horses in it was the thought that it would be cheaper to keep them at home. Boarding two horses was not then, and is not now, a cheap proposition, but we learned rather quickly, and it has been reconfirmed over the years, that keeping them at home isn't cheap either. Of course, as the number of horses rises, and the number of people working part-time or full-time in the barn goes up in proportion, the cost rises inexorably.

It used to be said of yachts that the cost of keeping one was like digging a bottomless pit and trying to fill it with money, and much the same thing can be said of the cost of running a barn— it absorbs money the way blotting paper absorbs moisture.

If you're planning to keep only one horse, and look after it yourself without any paid help, that's one thing, but that was never in the cards for us, and still isn't, if only because we were then going to be away in the city five days a week, and didn't necessarily suppose that this would change for a long, long time. In any event, putting the horses right opposite the front door was, as it turned out, one of those decisions which shifted the balance of our lives rather more suddenly than either of us might have anticipated. In Margaret's case, her old cat, Irving, might go back and forth in the car with us every weekend (though he didn't like the journey much), but the horses weren't going to be traveling with us, and Margaret was used to seeing her horses more than two days a week. In fact, so long as we lived in the city, we had always ridden together every day, whatever the weather, and whatever else was going on in our lives. We did not, immediately, take easily to becoming "weekend riders," Margaret least of all, so moving the horses to our own stable had the effect, for obvious reasons, of turning the house from a mere weekend home to a more central position in our lives. Without any definite decision to alter it, our center of gravity had shifted from Manhattan to ninety miles north of New York City.

Of course there *are* people who can leave their horses at home "in the country" and go off on world tours or extended business trips or skiing vacations with perfect peace of mind, and come back knowing that the horses have been looked after, exercised, trained, and kept ready at a moment's notice for the return of their owners. But these are mostly the very rich, the kind of people who can phone from their own jet to the barn manager and say, "We're on our way in from Aspen, and we'll go riding after breakfast tomorrow morning." Most of us don't live that sort of life, and those who do probably don't need a book on how to look after horses.

Since our two horses were being boarded at Katherine Boyer's farm, perhaps five miles away as the crow flies, and since at the time we moved them home we still didn't have a trailer, or, indeed, even a vehicle suitable for towing one, we decided to ride them home. This was by no means a feat of endurance, for them or for us; the major difficulty lay in finding our way along hunt trails, which seemed to zigzag endlessly and lead us from time to time across totally unfamiliar roads. Katherine Boyer's directions had been characteristically crisp and clear, but one hunt trail looks pretty much like another, and neither of us would have been altogether surprised had we arrived, after a couple of hours, back where we had started from, only to be told sharply by Katherine that we had paid insufficient attention to her directions.

In the end, that proved, very fortunately, to be unnecessary. We made our way along trails that would soon become familiar, past houses and farms that would eventually become landmarks, circling ever closer to our house, then crossed a small stream that appeared on the map that had accompanied the deeds to the house, crested a steep little hill past rusting remnants of what had once been wire fencing for sheep or cattle, and emerged onto the land right behind our stable, where Roxie was waiting in front of the barn door, a big smile on her face, ready to introduce the horses to their new home.

The horses didn't fuss about changing their residence. Roxie took off their tack, gave them her standard treatment, then turned them out into what was at the time our only paddock, where they settled in calmly.

In some ways, the first months of keeping the horses at home in our own barn were halcyon days. We went for long rides, exploring the land around us and gradually beginning to push farther and farther cross-country on the hunt trails. The two horses didn't dominate our life then. Every once in a while we could walk across the driveway, or get out of the car, and go look at the horses to make sure they were alright, and perhaps give them a sugar cube or a piece of carrot, but pretty soon they became part of the landscape, and it became hard to remember a time when they *weren't* there, or when the barn was used for the storage of the previous owners' debris.

We had always assumed that the stable would be an attraction for guests, and that the first thing they'd want to do on arrival, after having washed up and had a cup of coffee, would be to take a quick tour of the stable and see the horses, but this turned out not to be the case, for the most part. The few horse people we knew were eager enough to see (and criticize) our stable, and make the acquaintance of our horses, but most guests coming up from the city had to be dragged kicking and screaming to tour the stable, as if it were an unfamiliar or threatening environment, for which they had brought no suitable clothes or footwear. Inevitably, these visitors eyed both the horses and the floor cautiously, as if at any moment they might be bitten, or put a well-shod foot down in horse manure. We kept a supply of "horse treats" in the tack room, in fact, for the purpose of introducing house guests and horses, but until we had actually moved the horses home, neither of us realized how few people we knew had ever been in a stable, or stood close to a horse, let alone how few of them actually *wanted* to. Most retreated back to the house with a sigh of relief as quickly as possible for a strong drink, and definitely a good wash-up if they had touched—my God!—one of the horses!

People who own horses always assume that everybody wants to see them, but, as is the case with children, this is not invariably true, and the assumption that arriving guests want to leap right out of their car in their city clothes to admire the horses has gotten many a weekend off to a sticky start. In addition, of course, many of the things guests *would* like to see, like a swimming pool or a tennis court, are probably not going to be there because all the money went into the stable, the paddocks and so on—unless you're rich enough to have all three.

Of course the other big problem is that of guests who want to go riding, even though they may not have been on a horse for twenty years or more. Our horses were and remain very *personal,* which is to say that they are neither the kind of nice, broad-backed, easy-going old plugs on which you could put anyone without hesitation, nor the kind of horses you would necessarily want to risk in anyone else's hands. We didn't want an injured guest or horse. In Margaret's case, the horses she competes on play far too important a part in her life to let any stranger ride them, and in Michael's case, he has always tended to own the kind of horse that you have to know a little about before mounting, and about which you'd think twice before putting somebody whose riding abilities you weren't sure of in the saddle.

Gently—if necessary, *forcibly*—discouraging guests from the idea that they're going to ride with us may be perhaps one of the many reasons why our guest rooms are seldom in use now, but the truth is that just because the horses are at home doesn't mean that we feel like lending them out to people whose riding skills are an unknown quantity, nor that we want to conduct the equivalent of trail rides, nor should anybody else who decides to keep their horse(s) at home feel obliged to do so.

The sight of some woman friend from the city in skintight blue jeans and inappropriate boots (high heeled and also laced or zipped skin tight) cheerfully determined to go for a ride in the morning with us was one of the many reasons we clung to our habit of riding very early in the morning, long before any of our guests was likely to be awake. We took, in fact, to waking at the crack of dawn on Saturday and Sunday, if we had guests in the house, creeping around the kitchen in stocking feet trying not to make any noise while we fed the cats and emptied the dishwasher, so we could escape to the barn while everybody else in the house slumbered on. Often, when we came back to the barn after our ride it was to find a guest looking like Medea with a mug of coffee in hand waiting for us as we dismounted, having mistakenly formed the impression the night before, over the second or third glass of wine, that we would like nothing better than to provide a horse for her and take her riding with us. (For some reason most of our male guests had no desire to ride, but instead wanted to know why we didn't have a pool or a tennis court and why the Sunday *New York Times* wasn't delivered to our doorstep.) This kind of social embarrassment is the sort of thing you will simply have to get used to, if you're going to keep your horses at home.

In those more innocent days, we didn't worry that much about insurance and lawsuits and so on. These days, it may be possible to get out of this kind of social problem simply by saying that your insurance won't cover the risk of a guest riding one of your horses, which, as it happens, is more than likely to be true. It's also worth bearing in mind that the tradition of guests not suing their host (or hostess) is also long since gone, alas. There was recently a piece in the paper about a guest at somebody's house suing for (and collecting) millions because the carving knife slipped in her host's hand at the Thanksgiving dinner table and sliced her wrist badly—so you can imagine what she might have done had she fallen from one of his horses and hurt herself.

In any event, our own solution was to simply harden our hearts to this kind of thing, unless the person was somebody whose riding skills we knew and admired—seldom the case, as it happened, among our guests. Still, it's one of the odd things about having horses. People who would never think of asking you to lend them your treasured vintage Porsche or your favorite golf clubs, assume as a matter of course that you'll put them on a horse and send them (or take them) for a ride over the countryside. Those of us who own horses, on the other hand, are constantly aware of just how easy it is to injure them, or lose a shoe by trotting a horse through thick mud, or undo months of careful training by putting an unknowledgeable person in the saddle, and are therefore resistant to their being ridden by anybody we aren't completely sure of, or to have them treated as part of a weekend's hospitality, like the horses in a riding camp.

So long as we only had two horses at home, sharing them with guests was no problem, really. We each rode our own, and that was that. We blithely recommended to guests that they go antique hunting instead (this was a particularly good tactic because the nearest towns with even halfway decent antique

shops are many miles away, so we not only had the horses to ourselves, but even had the *house* to ourselves during most of the
day). When Margaret eventually moved her old Thoroughbred
Tabasco home from the place he was being boarded—a kind of
retirement home for horses that had not lived up to her expecta-
tions—we were in trouble, since to anybody who could count we
now had a "spare" horse. Very fortunately, Tabasco's personality,
even his appearance, did not inspire instant confidence in most
would-be riders. A big, handsome (even flashy) chestnut geld-
ing, Tabasco, despite his considerable age, was built for speed
and looked it, and while he was, in fact, a very sweet horse, especially toward Margaret whom he loved, with strangers his manner was at once nervous and intimidating. He was impatient
with riders who dithered or dawdled, and capable of a sudden
spook, stop, or buck that could send the unwary rider flying over
his head. On the rare occasions when a guest stubbornly insisted
on riding, and had enough experience so that it was hard to say
no, Tabasco usually made sure they never asked to go out riding
with us a second time.

Of course, the more horses you have, the more pressure
there will be from people to ride them, but very few horse owners, not even those wealthy enough to keep a lot of horses, are
usually happy about allowing guests to ride them. The key is to
have a firm policy on the subject and stick to it. In any event,
there is nothing like the sight of a guest on one of *your* horses
cantering across a field without even looking out for holes, or
trotting over rocks without slowing down and allowing the

horse to pick its way, or bringing a horse back in a muck sweat and winded, to convince even the most generous and hospitable of hosts that it's a bad idea to let somebody talk you into putting them on a horse of yours. Pay no attention at all to people who "spent their whole childhood riding," since it usually ain't so—and on this subject almost everybody gilds the lily. The truth is they have had many years in which to forget whatever they may have learned as children.

The likelihood is that guests whom you allow to ride will dismount, go into the house for a cup of coffee and leave somebody else to worry about cleaning the horse and the tack, but, annoying as that may be, it's in some ways better than the kind of guest who wants to help out in the barn, but doesn't know how. Watching somebody splash water all over your favorite saddle, or give a horse a quick "once over" with a brush or a towel, or upset your routine in any one of a hundred ways, is the kind of thing that quickly leads to a broken friendship. Generally speaking, the more eager people are to help, the more likely they are to simply be in the way, so that you will have to sneak back to the barn later on, while everybody else is having a drink before lunch, and redo everything they did the way you would have done it in the first place.

The important thing to remember is that the real reason for keeping your horse at home instead of boarding it is, in the final analysis, being able to control how it's looked after, and, perhaps just as important, having things done *your* way, even if you have to do them yourself. Certainly it's more work (maybe more than

you imagined), certainly it's a big responsibility, certainly it isn't cheap or easy, but the fact that Margaret has placed on the door a sign that reads, My Barn, My Rules, says it all—doing it your own way is what it's all about.

Doing it her own way was something that took a while for Margaret to achieve since, in our case, Roxie had her own agenda and set of priorities, as well as years of professional experience in looking after horses. For some time, the sign might as well have read, My Barn, Roxie's Rules. Roxie was an indefatigable worker, totally devoted to our horses and utterly reliable, but she did not take kindly to change, suggestions or interference with her routine. This, we would eventually discover, is the problem with barn help—the really good ones, who know what they're doing, don't want to be told what to do, while the ones who *don't* mind being told what to do are only too often ignorant or incompetent.

Adding Tabasco brought us up to three horses, of course. The difference between two horses and three does not seem a significant one, or a big decision, but in fact it's a crucial step. Once you start expanding, it is very difficult to *stop* the process, or even slow it down. Like everything else in life, "*Il n'ya que le premier pas qui coûte*" ("It's only the first step that's difficult"), as the Marquise du Deffand said of the martyred St. Denis, who is believed to have walked two leagues carrying his severed head in his hands. Roxie, it has to be said, was as eager to have Tabasco at home as Margaret was—there was no difficulty there—but a barn with three horses is an inevitably different proposition from a barn with two. When Richard rebuilt the old barn, giving us six stalls, we had never assumed that we would use them—after all we only had two horses—but now it was half-full (or, looked at in another way, half-empty), and it is a well known fact that nature abhors a vacuum.

Horse people abhor a vacuum too, particularly in the barn, and no horse person in his or her right mind is likely to let a stall remain empty for long, or lose an opportunity of filling it. Although the arrival of each new horse naturally meant more work for Roxie, she was as eager to fill the empty stalls as we were—she too kept her eyes open for likely candidates, especially as Margaret began to take up competing.

This too is a consideration when keeping horses at home. What purpose will they serve? A simple barn in which you keep one or two horses for the occasional "trail ride" is a very different proposition from one in which the horses are prepared for any kind of serious competition. There is not only bound to be more work, in terms of preparation, as well as almost automatically, the need for a trailer and a ring in which to practice and train. Far from raising any objection to any such schemes for expansion, Roxie treated them with enthusiasm—she was all for Margaret's competing, and indeed looked forward to competing herself.

Thus the usual brake on expanding the number of horses in the barn—"Not enough help," or "The help wouldn't stand for it," or whatever—didn't apply in our case. The help was as eager to see the barn grow and the horses compete as Margaret was, and in no time at all, it seemed, we went from having a two-horse barn to a four-horse barn and, eventually, to a five- or six-horse barn.

The early years of keeping the horses at home had a certain idyllic quality to them, which is well portrayed in photographs of the period. As we gradually acquired more land and hacked away at the trails (Harold Roe did the hacking, and much else besides), we discovered more and more places we wanted to clear.

Clearing land was, very fortunately, exactly the kind of job that Harold lived for, since it was endless (adding up to many, many hours of well-paid labor with a tractor and a bush-hog), required no fancy work like gardens or borders or areas around the house, which bored him, and could be undertaken without any supervision or interruption from us, since the field was a good long way from the house, and required crossing a stream. Here, left to himself, with a Thermos flask and a bar of chocolate, Harold could spend many a happy and remunerative day from dawn to dusk, bush-hogging, using his battery of chain saws, and working away at the roots of small trees with his backhoe. From the barn or the house the only indication of his presence somewhere out there in the landscape was the occasional screech of a chain saw and a steady, throbbing sound from the diesel engine of his tractor reverberating in the far distance.

Since Harold usually contrived to head out on the trails while we were still at breakfast and to return in the dark just as we were sitting down for dinner, it was hard to waylay him for a progress report, but eventually, when it was done to his satisfaction, we sloshed across the stream (Harold had already developed ambitious plans to build a bridge over it, which he later completed), down a rocky, muddy path, crested a low rise, and were delighted with what we saw.

Those were the days when keeping the horses did not seem like a chore, and when their presence, seen or unseen, seemed to fit naturally into the pattern of country living. Those were the days, when we actually *read* the Sunday paper, and went to movies in the afternoon, and sat outside with guests—the days before the barn came to take more and more time, with an ever increasing cast of characters to run it, and an ever lengthening list of chores and problems to take care of, and when, not incidentally, we had two or three horses, instead of five or six. One vaguely remembers going out to show them to guests, drinks in hand, and trying to encourage "city people" to feel at pleasure being up close with horses, and offering the horses an apple, or one of those "horse cookies," before going in to loll on the beautifully decorated porch for a while longer before dinner . . .

Well, but that's one of things to learn about keeping horses at home—what starts out as a hobby, as *fun,* can easily take over your life, so it helps to start out with a pretty firm idea of how far

Margaret, Michael, Caroline, and Murry Ramson, celebrating the joy of owning one's own barn, Stonegate Farm, early 1980's. (Note the "Secretariat" fencing.)

you want to go, and how much time you're prepared to give it, and who is going to help you do it, when and if you need help. It's very easy to let it grow until it's become the equivalent of a full-time job, and then some, and also easy to forget that in certain parts of the country (ours, for instance) what seems like a real breeze in the summer is an altogether different story when snow is falling at a couple of inches an hour on top of big banks of snow that one hasn't cleared away yet from the last storm, when the plunging thermometer threatens to freeze the pipes, and when the horses' paddocks begin to resemble skating rinks. At that point in time it's usually too late to throw one's hands up in the air, say, "To hell with it," and leave for Florida. But at its best, the first years of our having our horses at home were ones we remember with pleasure, when we look back at them, and indeed many of the photographs of that time *do* have a kind of warm, surreal glow, with the horses in the background, rather than in the foreground, as problems.

Of course we were spoiled for some time, particularly since Richard and Roxie never seemed to take vacations themselves, lulling us into the belief that they would always be on hand. Once Roxie had her first child, however—she rode up until the day her water broke, and could only be persuaded with great difficulty to give up jumping—the Bacons became a family, and started to behave a little more like one, which meant they began to take a regular vacation. Fortunately, this took place in the summer—the idea of a winter vacation had not presented itself to them—but at least it had the advantage of giving us a taste of what running the barn would be like *without* Roxie. (Attempts to find people who would replace her during her vacations also gave us an insight into just how hard it is to find competent, *reliable* people to do barn work—a problem which was exacerbated by Roxie's groundless fear that anybody who replaced her during her vacation might eventually replace her altogether, or, only slightly better, might alter or rearrange the way she kept things in the barn—and which we would eventually solve by bringing Margaret's goddaughter Tamzin over from England.

All the same, the early years of keeping horses, were, in their way, almost misleadingly idyllic, with Margaret and Tamzin sunning themselves on the lawn behind the barn in the long afternoons, looking out at the horses, or Margaret in her bikini striding down toward the "Powerline Field" to collect her horses and bring them home, or, bikini-clad, lunging Tabasco on the lawn.

The thing is, the barn *worked*. Somehow it fit organically into our lives, into the landscape of our home, which it defined and formed, and gave identity to the place we had chosen to live, so that it was no longer, in fact, a house, but really *a farm*. It was not, needless to say, a *profitable* farm, or even a professionally run farm, but with fields, fences, stable, manure pile and, above all, horses, it was indubitably a real farm, as opposed to all those country houses owned by city people (in our part of the country) that are always called "Cherrystone Farm," or whatever, but on which no recognizable agricultural activity ever takes place, or would be allowed to, beyond landscape gardening, which is usually contracted out to somebody.

Making a profit out of running a horse farm is notoriously difficult—for example, you can board other people's horses, in which case you have to provide at least certain limited facilities for them, or you have to buy and sell horses, a business which requires the combined instincts of a used-car dealer and a sports promoter if it's going to bring in a steady revenue. We have several neighbors who board other people's horses, but in every case one of the spouses has a well paying job (or has "family money"), so they're not living off the business. Happily for us, the idea of making a profit never occurred to us at first. The object of having the horses at home in our own barn was to please ourselves, and that turned out to be hard enough to do without also trying to make money at it.

Early on in the game, however, our friend and business adviser, Jay Watnick, watching the checks go out, fluttering away like autumn leaves for things which seemed to him mysterious or puzzling (fencing, hay and feed, farrier, vet bills, the indoor ring . . .) suggested how useful it would be to turn the barn into a *business,* and find a way to make it profitable, or at least to produce enough income to make some of the expenses legitimately tax-deductible. Jay and his wife, Marianna, even came up to spend the weekend and have a look at the barn themselves. There must be *some* way, they suggested, in which it could produce an income.

We went through our usual litany: we didn't want to board other people's horses, or buy and sell horses. . . .

"How about *breeding* horses?" Marianna said. "Margaret loves animals, she'd get a kick out of that, surely?"

But breeding horses was the one thing having to do with the horse world that Margaret *didn't* want to do, never mind that, at that time, our horse population consisted of three geldings. Breeding takes a huge amount of time and a high degree of specialized knowledge, in addition to which it's another of those businesses which usually requires a considerable degree of subsidizing. Rather than a way to make a profit, breeding horses is, for most people, either an expensive hobby, or a tax write-off, or a way of absorbing excess income, like art collecting or keeping a large seagoing yacht with a full crew. Neither of us had the slightest wish to do it, nor could we see even the faintest prospect of making a profit—on the contrary, the only result would have been an even bigger blizzard of checks going out, still with none coming in.

The Watnicks were not persuaded. There must be some way to create an income, they insisted.

Why should that be the case, we asked? They had a pool at their house in the country. Did it produce an income? They didn't rent their pool out to strangers in the summers, or organize swimming competitions and charge so much a head. Our barn was like their pool—though, as they were quick to point out, the expenses of keeping a pool were a lot less than those of keeping horses, and you could close it down and forget about it from Labor Day to Memorial Day.

Other visitors from the city echoed their thoughts, with suggestions for everything from pony rides, to boarding circus horses during the winter, in search of a way to make the barn "a profit center," but nothing anybody ever mentioned seemed practical, or even feasible, to us. Eventually, Margaret persuaded a local farmer to hay our fields, which sometimes produced pretty decent hay, but not much in the way of cash income. Then the farmer injured himself in one of those ghastly accidents involving agricultural machinery that explains why farming is still considered to be the most dangerous occupation in the United States, and had to give it up. Since the fields still had to be mown if we were going to ride over them, and since nobody seemed to want our hay, we had to pay somebody to do it, which moved it from the profit to the debit side of the ledger. Our hay had never amounted to much anyway, except in Jay's imagination. There *is* a living to be made out of hay and straw, as anybody who has ever bought a load of either can attest, but it requires an awful lot of hay and straw, as well as the ability to deliver tons of it to where it's wanted, and, if possible, half a dozen or so muscular teenaged sons to stack it and move it.

Later, and more successfully, Margaret hit upon the idea of holding her own cross-country schooling trials on our land, but if you included time, labor, and the expense of building ever more elaborate and solid cross-country jumps, you couldn't even break even. Essentially, all these income-producing schemes had in common, however, the fact that they were not really connected to the barn itself, or to our own horses, but merely represented different ways of using our land. You might break even on a big one-day cross-country event, if you were lucky and the weather was on your side, but it wouldn't go far in paying for the expense of keeping the barn going for our own horses, nor, as we never tired of explaining to our business adviser and to Stuart Yontef, our accountant, had we ever supposed it would. The barn might be central to our lives, but it was still a *hobby,* not a paying business, and no more likely to pay for itself than any other complicated, demanding, and expensive hobby.

Particularly difficult to explain was that given Margaret's relationship to her horses, there was no likelihood of our going into the business of selling horses, even if we had been equipped to make money out of it (doubtful in the first place). Her horses were like her children, and once they arrived in our barn they were likely to stay for life, however old and crippled they got, and however high their vet bills became, or the cost of sustaining them on special feeds, nutrients, and regular treatments of acupuncture. It was like looking for a way to make money out of your own children.

Thus, we accepted, almost from the beginning, that keeping the horses at home was one of the built-in expenses of the life we had chosen, rather than the beginning of an interesting tax scheme or a thriving small business, and faced the fact, however little sense it made to anybody else (particularly to those who lived in New York City), that the barn was one of the things we were working *for*. Occasionally, as the years went by, we would have occasional serious discussions about "cutting back," or reducing the cost, or eliminating the frills, but these seldom led to any serious change. The horses were *there*, first two, then three, then five or six, and they had to be fed, groomed, shod, cared for, and housed, and that was that. Where other people yearned (and worked) for a beach house in the Hamptons, our spare cash, such as it was, went toward new fields, fencing, barn, and horses, and on many days, when the weather was good, and we had a good long ride out of our own barn, and over our own land (and perhaps our neighbors'), it mostly seemed like a sensible decision.

On days when the thermometer dropped well below freezing, snowstorms howled in from Canada or Buffalo, and water turned to ice as you filled a bucket, the decision did not always seem quite as sensible as it did on a clear, sunny day in June. From time to time—when horses went lame or became seriously ill, when barn help failed to arrive or threw tantrums, when the vet bills seemed to be more expensive than our own medical bills could ever be—we questioned it more severely. But nearly a quarter of a century later, the barn is still there, as we write this, and the current barn population of four horses are outside in their fields grazing (not quite as idyllic a picture as it looks from the distance, admittedly, since one of them is an old-age pensioner by now), and it's so impossible to imagine what our lives would be like *without* all that out there, that any discussion about it seems to lead nowhere, or to a blank area in the imagination which neither of us can fill. The barn and the horses are part of our lives, and, apparently, that's that.

Indeed that, rather than bankruptcy or physical exhaustion, may be the ultimate danger in keeping your horse or horses at home. They become a permanent fixture of your life, the raison d'être for living in the country or having a country house, impossible to explain or justify to others, or to give up, the center around which your own life revolves. It's not just a question of obsession—lots of unremunerative activities are obsessional, after all—it's that the horse is a living being, ownership of which helps to define who you are. The ancient Scythians—horsemen and -women of the great Mongolian plains—measured their wealth in horses, worshipped horse-like gods, did business in solid gold pieces made in the shape of horses, and were buried together with their favorite horses so they would not be without them in the afterlife. The last is probably further than the modern horse lover will want to go (or will be allowed to go by funeral directors and the law), but the point is that our relationship with our horses is simultaneously deeply felt and deeply personal, and once they are at home with us, they are, so to speak, kin, as well as valuable personal possessions, and correspondingly hard to give up.

Just as the ancient Scythian planted his tent in the middle of his horse herd, once you move your horse or horses home to your own barn, they are part of your life. So be warned, once you start, it won't be easy to stop, close down the barn, and send them away. You're stepping into "big magic" here, as Native Americans called anything that was deeply personal and elemental, which, for the Plains Indians too, included the horse, an animal that they both used and worshipped, and painted in designs and colors that matched their own individual "war paint" so that man and beast merged into one entity.

Having your own horses at home with you is a link to one of humanity's oldest and most powerful obsessions. The horse always added power, wealth, speed, beauty, physical grace, and nobility to man, and the ownership of horses, the sight of one's own horses in one's own fields, has been the pinnacle of man's social ambitions and claim to aristocratic heritage for too many centuries to count. On the great Egyptian temples, built four or five thousand years ago, there is scene after scene, carved in stone, and once gilded and painted, of Pharaohs inspecting their stables and admiring their horses (though they rode behind them, in a chariot, as opposed to riding *on* them); so the desire to do that is hardly new, or a novelty, and indeed was already old before the building of the Pyramids. Even in the days when the palaces of nobles and kings were made of clay bricks and mud, one wing of the structure was always, recognizably, designed as a stable, so we are dealing here with an old and potent form of measuring wealth, importance, and self-esteem, as well as respect and affection for the animal itself.

Keep in mind too that looking after horses isn't exactly new. The hoof pick in roughly its present form was known and in daily use at the time the Pyramids were being built, some six thousand years ago—there are samples of them in the museum at Cairo. Horse care, and a good, sound routine for looking after horses, go back to the dawn of civilized human life—the basic principles don't have to be reinvented and haven't changed appreciably since long before the stirrup was invented.

Given this, however, it's surprising how many people don't know, or can't be bothered to follow, the fairly simple rules for keeping the horse healthy and functioning. Some version of Margaret's stable rules was no doubt inscribed in Pharaoh's stables, as well as those of the Roman emperors, and those who followed them. Of course veterinary medicine has taken huge leaps forward (in tandem with human medicine), and of course everything from space age adhesives to Velcro to a vast array of prescription medications and food supplements have dramatically changed certain aspects of horse care, but basic facts, like keeping a horse's bedding clean and dry will prevent hoof ailments like thrush (as well as most of the cures for thrush once the horse gets it) have been around, as we say in England, since "the year dot."

In any case, once we had the horses at home, our lives were permanently changed, in ways we could scarcely have foreseen. Who, for example, would ever have dreamed, when we lived on Central Park West, overlooking the park, and gave black-tie dinner parties for twelve people, that the manure pile would eventually play a major role in our lives?

Chapter Four

The Barn Routine

There is much that is sublime about horses and horse keeping, but some of the basics are unavoidable, and not sublime at all. Some things are constants and part of the routine, such as the fact that horses produce manure—and soiled bedding, and more manure. Manure was an escapable presence in life until the First World War, when the mass production of the automobile caused manure to be replaced by the noxious exhaust gasses that have given us smog, global warming, and acid rain instead. Our ancestors did not give a lot of thought to manure—you walked through it, or around it, or paid people to brush it out of your way, and that was that. In the country, it was gathered in carts and spread on the fields—"mucked"—to enrich the soil, and the smell was widely assumed to be a healthy one. In the city it was swept up with brush and shovel, and carted away, a menace in the days when a lady's skirt trailed along the ground.

However, if you're going to keep horses, or even just one horse, it's something you have to think about—maybe the *first* thing you have to think about, in fact. As you will discover, there is no ideal solution. Put it too far away from the barn, and it's hard to get to it, put too near, and it makes its presence known; put it too far from the road and it's going to be hard to get it trucked away.

In any event, it's a reality, and not only hard to ignore, but harder to ignore with every day that goes by.

Believe it or not, Margaret points out, this is a major question when thinking about having your own barn and horses. "I knew some people who had redone an existing barn and small indoor, down to the last detail, but could never agree upon where to put the manure—and this ended up being such a bone of contention, that in the end, a horse never set hoof on the place!

"Location is very important. Out of sight but not too far away. But I am afraid that there will be days when wherever it is, the aroma will hang in the air. I remember many years ago, some friends who had been wanting to come and visit our new country place, finally arrived, stepped out of their car, held up their faces to breathe in some of that wonderful crisp fall air, and almost immediately froze, 'What is that dreadful smell?' Ah well. . . .Our manure pile is out of sight, and slightly behind paddock #11 (see map on page 33). We eventually blacktopped the narrow pathway from the barn to it, as this made it easier to snowblow in the winter, and the smoother ride meant less spillage of the overflowing wheelbarrow.

"There are several ways one can go about taking care of the manure. In the very early days, Harold Roe, who had a manure spreader, did just that—he spread it over some of the fields. We would dump it in an area, which he had constructed, with three retaining walls—ours are wooden, but concrete is very common too. And when there was what Harold considered an amount worth the trouble of hitching up his spreader, then that's what he would do. Later he made a 'manure pile' on top of one of the hilly fields, but he was never happy with this solution, worrying about it leaching into the water table, and stopped that rather abruptly. Still, since we used only straw in those days, there was no problem, as the many mushroom farmers would come and happily take all we had.

"I often wonder what happened to all those farmers? Suddenly they vanished. So since then, and with the increasing use of shavings, we had to look for another solution. It's now hauled away about four to five times a year. It means finding someone with a front loader and a good size truck. And depending on how much there is to be moved, it can take a few hours or even a day. Try to get a price fixed ahead of time for doing this! As we have to haul out through paddock #11, we are always very careful to plan as well as we can, for the ground to be as hard as possible, and try to avoid wet weather ahead of time and rain on the day. Otherwise the paddock will get pretty messed up with the truck going backward and forward. But you must not get caught going into winter with a huge load of manure on hand, as we did once, due to weather—almost six months' worth accumulated before it could be moved.

"Many places have a Dumpster in a location nearby to the barn, but for this you need some form of a ramp, as you will need to run the wheelbarrow up the ramp in order to get its contents into the dumpster, and a regular collection date, depending on the number of horses in the barn—and time of year. Ordinarily when one dumpster is collected, another is delivered.

"In England it is quite common to burn your 'muck heap,' as it is called there. I have expert advice on this method from my old school friend, Nancy Blinkhorn, who says that it is best if burned daily, so that it does not last too long, and therefore smell too long! And of course the wind direction is vitally important—blowing away from home! Wet hay and shavings smell the worst, straw not so bad. Her daughter, my goddaughter, Tamzin, would not hesitate to say, 'It stinks; it's disgusting. Over the years I think she has lost her sense of smell!' Oh, and should you ever go and live in England and have horses at home, you do not need a permit from the local council to burn; and try and find a friendly farmer who will come and take away the ash, once a year, so you can start from scratch annually.

"Of course I am sure that many people have other ways of 'unloading' their manure. I know of one person, who has two horses, who picks up her one paddock every day, as well as cleaning three stalls, puts it all into muck buckets, loads it onto an old truck—kept for just that purpose—and drives it a half mile down the country road, where a local farmer lets her tip it out in one of his fields. That's a tiring task at the end of every day, throughout the year, whatever the weather.

"One last word on the subject! Keep the area around the manure pile tidy, raked up, mow the grass around it, weedwack the weeds, and have good sturdy planks nearby, since you will need them as it grows higher and you have to run the wheelbarrow farther out to empty it. Manure piles are not a thing of beauty by any standards, so I have found that anything you can do to keep them from being an eyesore, is worth doing."

Once you've sited your manure pile, which is priority one, you can start figuring out how you're going to look after these horses. Of course there are a lot of ways to do that, but basically there are only a couple of choices: with barn help, or without barn help, is the first one; and the second one is whether to develop some kind of solid daily routine that works for you, or attempt to do it in chaos. We never actually had to make either of these choices—we had Roxie, and Margaret is by nature an orderly person (and Roxie still more so), so the best thing to do is to let Margaret describe what our barn routine was, and, with some modifications, still is.

A word of explanation. We do not pretend our way is the *only* way. When Michael served in the British armed forces, sergeants were inclined to tell recruits, "There are three ways to do things; the right way, the wrong way, and *my* way," followed by a meaningful pause, then: "We're going to do things *my* way." We are not suggesting anything like that, we're simply going to describe how *we* do it, in the hope that you'll find it useful, or at least consoling. There may be better ways—no doubt there are—but this is what we do at Stonegate Farm.

Margaret's Barn Routine

"At Stonegate Farm we have a set routine," Margaret says. "I function best within a structure, but this does change at certain times of the year—spring and fall, for severe weather conditions, or in the event of an emergency. And, during my eventing season. It may not be possible for others to keep to a schedule as we do here, for many reasons. Perhaps they like the idea of 'doing' their barn/horses, when they feel like it, when it suits them; they may not be morning people; they may have a full-time or part-time job; they may travel, and need part-time help when they are away, who come to take care of your horses when their hours allow them. But I have found that if you are able, horses are best when on a fixed routine.

"Changes in the regular routine come about for the following reasons:

1. In the winter all our horses, with the exception of one, are in at night, unless we have an unusually mild winter with no ice, as we did a couple of years ago, and they are not standing in water. I am very comfortable with them being out at night, as we have run-in sheds and automatic waters, and they are well blanketed. By mid April they go out twenty-four hours a day until the bugs get bad. Then they come in all day and are out all night,

until mid September, when they will go back out for twenty-four hours a days until we get bad weather, which for me, means ice on the ground.

2. In the case of severe weather conditions, a winter storm, or continuous torrential rain and flooding, which we saw in the summer of '03, I will bring horses in at night in the summer rather than having them stand in water—their feet will suffer and your blacksmith will have no hoof to nail a shoe to. And this change in routine will mean you will have to play around with your normal turn-out schedules, so the horse is not continually in for several days—a very bad idea, at any time of the year for horses who are unused to being stall bound. Even in winter, whatever the weather, my horses always go out in the morning and unless we get a really bad storm, they do not come in before their usual time.

3. An emergency can throw everything out of whack, and if it is horse-related you may be dealing with it yourself, or waiting for the vet. If person-related, you can be left shorthanded. Weather can cause delays for your help if they don't live on the premises, and those delays will spill over into the start and the end of the day.

4. When I am competing, it usually alters the course of the day. Horse(s) will usually be in overnight; the people going with me will be here at least one and a half to two hours before we leave, depending on what needs to be done; and on many occasions we will be loaded and gone long before the start of a normal day.

"I have a riding list and a turn-out list in the barn, made up the day, or days ahead, so tack can be set up the evening before, ready for the morning, horses are fed—a good time saver! Horses not being ridden or ridden later, will be groomed first, have the appropriate turn-out blanket put on, and turned out, their morning hay taken with them. As the run-in sheds are cleaned out the afternoons of the previous day, the morning turnout is made easy. The automatic waters need checking, and we throw out the water sitting overnight, and let fresh run in. Horses that are first up for riding get a flake of hay in their stalls, while the others are being taken care of. Then they are groomed and tacked up. Grain is made up for the next feeding. Stalls get started. Once mucked, clean bedding is left banked up during the day; the floors are limed where necessary. Water buckets are scrubbed. Feed tubs are checked and wiped out. The stalls and aisle are dusted; the aisle is swept and sprinkled with a water and Pine-Sol solution. The hay/straw/shavings stall is swept clean, and all the 'construction' bags we use for carrying hay are tidied up into a pile. We keep a pair of wire cutters hanging on a hook in the hay stall, for cutting the wire or baling twine around the hay and straw bales. Hang on to the baling twine, it can be useful for various things, and always remove any nails or hooks before using the stall for a horse. Stable sheets and coolers are hung on racks and covered with large towels. It's an easy way to keep horse clothing clean, and towels can be put in the washing machine easier than stable sheets. The bedding is pulled back down in the afternoon and hay and water buckets are filled, unless it's very cold, and then not until the horses come in (with a mix of half cold and half hot water, to keep from freezing!).

"The horses come in by 4 p.m., are groomed, have their blankets changed, and have their afternoon feed at that time. Barn check is done at 8 p.m.—stalls are picked up, water buckets filled, and more hay given. And of course each horse gets checked.

"On the spring/fall schedule when the horses are out twenty-four hours a day, the stalls are stripped, washed down, and swept once a week; the barn is still dusted and the aisles swept each day. The run-in sheds are cleaned twice a day, morning and afternoon. And always cobwebbed once a day; you would be surprised how busy the spiders can be!

"As the spring grass comes, we start to rotate paddocks, moving onto the back ones, being careful of the amount of time we leave the horses on the new grass, until they become accustomed to it. The winter paddocks are allowed time to rest. This being the time of year that we use the least hay, we let the bales of hay dwindle down until the loft is empty, so it can be completely cleaned out, before the next load comes in. (Though it is swept every time hay is thrown down, the loose hay going to Juan's sheep or Peter's chickens.) But make sure that you have ordered well in advance—don't get caught empty-handed.

"On the summer schedule, when the horses are in during the day and out at night, they are brought in as soon as people get here, at 7:30 a.m., and are fed in their stalls, and are groomed after eating. As they generally are hosed off or washed down after being ridden in the summer, a light grooming is done in the afternoon. They either go out around 4 p.m. or if it's extremely hot and humid, we will keep them in until later. We have a box fan attached to the outside of each stall and one big aisle fan. Even though we have rubber mats in the stalls, during the summer when the flies bother the horses—and they stamp their feet all the time, no matter how often you flyspray them—I like to keep the bedding quite deep immediately inside the stall doors, as that is where they hang out most of the time. Stalls are mucked out in the late afternoon or early evening, same routine as winter, and again banked up until the following morning, limed, and buckets scrubbed, hay put in ready for the a.m. We have a summer barn check at 8 p.m., when they get hay if needed—usually not, as we have so much grass—and their water is checked. At this time, their fly masks are removed and, if dirty, I like them to be hosed off or put in a bucket of water and rinsed. I would strongly recommend doing this several times a week.

"For me, the barn routine also includes daily tack cleaning, keeping the laundry room swept and mopped, the tack and feed rooms dusted and vacuumed, and saddle pads, polo wraps, towels, etc., laundered. The area outside the barn where we have the mounting block and two sets of cross ties with 4-x-9-foot rubber mats between the posts, where all the grooming/bathing is done (except for the winter), needs to be blown clean with a leaf blower, and/or hosed off. And the path to the manure pile and the area surrounding the pile need raking up. Hay that has been dragged out of the run-ins, is raked up once, if not twice, a day. We use plastic 'construction' bags to carry hay out to the horses, in the back of the Gator, in a wheelbarrow, or over your shoulder. No mess, less work.

"Always a good thing."

CHAPTER FIVE

The Care of the Horse

The horse's own care and routine are equally important. Again, everybody has their own way of doing what needs to be done, but this is Margaret's. Note that once again, climate and the use you make of your horse or horses are important factors to consider.

As Margaret puts it, "Animals are creatures of habit, whether domestic or wild. True we have a strong hand in the routine of the domestic animal, but all the years that I lived in Kenya I watched wild animals hunt, sleep, visit watering holes, and migrate, on a rigid routine of their own making.

"As with my barn routine, the horses are in a very structured system. The routine seldom varies, unless I am away at horse trials, on vacation, in the city, or in the case of injury—to *them*, not me (things go on pretty much the same if I get hurt or am sick). Horses need to be handled quietly but firmly at all times, but especially when being groomed; a heavy-handed person can start many issues that will stay with the horse throughout its lifetime. The same when horses are being tacked up. It really annoys me when I see people yanking up a girth, or dragging the bit out of the horse's mouth when taking off the bridle. The correct way to do this is to first undo the throat latch, cavesson, and curb chain, if using a bit that requires one to. Stand at the near side of the horse's head, making sure the reins remain over the horse's neck, then place your left hand on the bridle where the browband and head-piece meet, and position your right arm under the horse's throat and, reaching up to the same area of the bridle on the side away from you, gently slip the bridle over the horse's head and ears, allowing the horse to open his mouth and the bit to slip out. Have a halter over your left arm before starting and put it on your horse before taking the reins over his head. I never have nylon, poly-web, or cotton web halters without breakaway leather crowns, and know horse owners who will only have leather halters in their barns.

"Our horses are fed at the same time each day; whether two meals, or more, keep to the same time, horses get immediately accustomed to when their feed is coming, and many can get more than a little impatient, if they are made to wait! Then, if they are in, their stable sheets will be brushed off while they are still in their stalls, which saves unnecessary mess in the aisle. Here, I would add that my horses' tails are never brushed or combed, which pulls the hair out— straw, hay, or shavings are carefully picked out by hand. When a horse has a bath, or just its mane and tail have been shampooed, then tails can be brushed out, but only after ShowSheen has first been sprayed on them. Their feet are picked out and their shoes checked. Next they get their major grooming of the day, which includes a good vacuuming. And the process will be repeated again in the late afternoon, throughout the year, whether they are in or out.

"When a horse first goes into its stall they will usually urinate within a minute or two. We catch the first pee in a bucket, as it is usually heavy and will stale the stall immediately. Roxie started this habit and I have kept it up throughout the years. The horses get used to you with the bucket very quickly, especially in the beginning if you have a small treat for them.

"Anytime their legs are muddy, we wash or hose them off, and dry them with towels. Wet or dry, do not ignore mud. And during muddy times, check to see if your horse(s) have any signs of scratches in the heel areas, which I treat with Desitin, with good results—just rub a little into the affected spot.

"Also the afternoon grooming of the day is a good time to oil their feet, if needed, during dry periods in summer and frozen winters. On the other hand, if your horses are standing in wet paddocks, keep an eye peeled for any signs of thrush. We use a product called 'Thrush Buster' and squirt a little in every four or five days, as a preventative measure. In addition we apply a product called 'Hoof Toughner' just below the coronary band and around the nail holes—there is no need to cover the entire foot.

"Special attention should be paid to checking for ticks, at least twice a day from early spring through fall. Many horses react strongly to tick bites, others less. A small amount of Ichthammol on the affected area is helpful, and a pair of tweezers kept in your grooming box can be used for pulling the ticks off.

"Anything that may have happened during the night or

daytime, whether in their stall or out, such as a scrape or cut, should be taken care of as soon as noticed. If it's serious, the horse's temperature* should be taken so when I talk to the vet, I can pass along that information, and take it from there as to whether a farm call is necessary or not."

"As I have mentioned previously, there is always a riding schedule for each day, made up ahead of time, as to who will be ridden, and at what time, and a general idea of what they will be doing: a hack, a dressage lesson, a stadium jumping or cross-country lesson, or interval training. This also lets your help know if anything different from the everyday equipment will be necessary, such as galloping boots, a different bit or saddle, or maybe studs for example. If you are going to use the same bridle on another horse, remember to rinse the bit between rides, and in the winter, warm the bit unless you are bringing the bridle from a heated tack room and tacking up straight away. Horses do not like ice cold metal put into their mouths, and you could start a problem.

"We usually begin riding at 8:30 a.m., unless the weather is extremely hot and humid in the summer, and never later than 10 a.m., and that would be if Michael and I had the chance to sleep in during the holidays. But for many horse owners, when they ride may be determined by other factors, or a personal choice of time.

"When each horse, or horses come back from being ridden, they will be brushed off, their feet checked and picked out again,

---

*Normal temperature ranges from 99 to 101. This may vary with individual horses, so it's a good idea to know your horse's baseline.

and a cooler will immediately be thrown over them if it's cold. In the hot weather, they will either be hosed off, or washed down with a sponge, a sweat scraper will take off the excess water, and then they will be fly-sprayed.

"Springtime is tough when they are shedding, and I have always found you can use a shedding blade to its best advantage after riding, when the horse is slightly warm. But walk your horse into a nearby paddock when you are going to do this, or you will have handfuls of old winter hair covering everything in sight. It's very important to make sure that if you are planning to pull a mane, or do something time consuming with a horse immediately after being worked, that you first take the horse onto some grass to allow them to urinate; ninety percent of the time they will.

"Then they are turned out for the day if it is winter, or day and night in the spring and fall. If not, they go into their stalls. And then, on to the next horse, or horses.

"If you have help, a good plan is to have them ready the next horse for you by the time you get back with the first set, if not, allow yourself a good forty-five minutes between rides, to untack, clean up, blanket if necessary, and turn out.

"Among the things I like to have all my horses do is to stand quietly at the mounting block and while you are opening and closing gates. It may take a little patience in the beginning, but stick with it. Get horses into the habit of being 'ponied' or being ridden while you are 'ponying' from them. This means, riding one and leading another at the same time. If you are short of time, or the weather is too cold to go out twice, this is a good way to get your horses exercised. Of course, should you have horses with bad habits that could cause problems when working close beside one another, do not do this. Horses usually get the hang of being 'ponied' quickly, and you just have to remember a few things: keep the head of the horse you are leading up by your knee, not dragging way behind you; don't wrap the lead line around your hand, hold in loose loops, this way should either horse get spooked or stumble, you will not end up in the emergency room waiting for a hand specialist.

"Have your horses become used to going out alone and in groups. When in company, it's a good thing if the horse you are riding can handle being left on its own, being behind the group, or being in the lead. If you have to get off for some reason, it's nice to have your horse stand still and let you get back on, either from the ground, or from something you can stand on. Usually if your horse has learned to stand at the mounting block, it will stand by a jump. There is nothing more aggravating, at that moment, than trying to get your foot into the stirrup while your horse is sidestepping or backing away from you.

"And horses must load without problems. Just because your horse arrived and unloaded just fine does not mean it will go back on the trailer! So should you have a problem with this, you will need practice. Never wait until you are all ready to leave for a show, or an event, or hunter pace, to find out if your horse will load. And even if you never plan to do anything but ride at home, you may still have to ship your horse in an emergency, when time is of the essence.

"My horses get their manes pulled regularly, and their 'bridle paths' and whiskers around their muzzles trimmed once a week. My friend Carol Kozlowski passed on a great tip: when pulling manes, wear latex gloves, they save wear and tear on your fingers. I am not a great lover of 'pulled' tails, as I seldom see it well done, and I cannot do a good job myself. So we leave our horses' tails alone, but do often braid for the dressage phase of an event. And we 'bang' the bottoms—a blunt cut—so they are even. For the best results, and I learned this from Carol too, first start with a clean and detangled tail, I would add here that she never uses anything but a human hairbrush on tails and starts at the bottom and works up to avoid breakage. Have a helper put an arm under the horse's dock to lift it in the position the horse would carry it if moving. Using a large pair of sharp scissors cut straight across at the desired length, just below the hocks, remembering not to take too much off as you can always trim later! Brush through and recut at the same place two or three times to get all the stray hairs. Then have someone lead the horse away so you can see it in motion, and make any adjustments. Recut every month to keep tidy. In the fall I will bang them shorter for the winter months, but let them grow longer in the spring. Be careful of allowing a tail to become too long. I have seen horses step backward, stand on their tails, and pull large amounts of the tail out. We keep their legs and fetlocks trimmed when needed from spring until fall, but do not touch them during the winter, nor do we trim their muzzles.

"I do not do much clipping here. Old horses like Missouri,

because of their age, need to be body clipped in the summer, and trace clipped at other times of the year. If I have a horse with a particularly thick coat, that is going to compete before he has shed out, then I will do it, and the same with some horses who have unnaturally thick coats—sometimes they need clipping in the summer to keep them comfortable. Remember before clipping to make sure the horse has had a good bath, or if it's winter, do the best you can to get him as clean as possible. You will get better results. Know what you are doing, and if you don't, find someone who does! Take care of your clipper blades. Keep them clean, oiled, and regularly sharpened. Always have a second set of blades. Clipping is a grubby job, so wear old clothes!

"Cleaning sheaths should also be a routine job. For some horses more often than others. A lot of horse owners have their vet do this, in which case the horse usually gets a small dose of tranquilizer. But we do not. The sheath is folded flaps of skin forming a sac that holds the penis. Use disposable gloves, and either a mild soapy detergent or one of the sheath cleaning products. I recommend the latter. I use Excalibur. Use warm water and wads of cotton, making sure that the area is well rinsed. Leaving any residue, especially if using a detergent, can cause dryness and irritation. Mares should be cleaned too. It's a less intrusive job but important during and after they have been in season.

"Don't forget your horses' teeth. Equine dental care is generally known as 'floating.' At least once a year either your vet, or if you prefer—and many horse owners do—an equine dentist, should examine the horse's mouth, teeth, and gums. Some horses need their teeth done every three to six months. We have an excellent equine dentist, who travels here from Pennsylvania. As we are a small barn we coordinate this with one or two other area barns on the same day. I know people who ship their horses long distances to have their teeth taken care of. It is an important part of good horse maintenance and should not be overlooked.

"All the horses are on a regular program for shots and worming. In late January, the vet draws blood for their Coggins Test, which checks for equine infectious anemia. You will need a certificate for a negative Coggins Test, and should carry it with you at all times when transporting a horse. I keep mine in an envelope in the glove compartment of my truck and another set in the tack room. Most shows will not accept your entries without an accompanying copy, and very few landowners/barn owners will allow you to unload your horse without one. An emergency facility would give priority to an emergency, but would definitely prefer a negative Coggins. At the same time the horses get their rabies shots, which can only be given by a veterinarian in New York and many other states. This would be a good time to draw blood for a rabies test, as you are required to enclose a copy of your rabies certificate along with entry forms for many shows and horse trials. The horses also get their strangles vaccine, which today is most often given in the form of a nasal spray. Intramuscular strangles vaccine is still available, but not as effective, and often associated with local vaccine reaction, which is a hot swollen area at the injection site.

"The remainder of the yearly shots we do ourselves. I would

like to strongly point out that no one should administer injections without first having a veterinarian show them how to do this, and then oversee them the first few times they do it. You should be aware that anytime you are giving vaccines there is a small risk of an anaphylactic reaction, which could lead to death. We pick up the vaccines from the vet a day or so before we plan to give the shots, and it's an important thing to know which need refrigeration and which do not. All my horses get the three-in-one shot in February; this is for Eastern/Western Encephalitis and Tetanus. The next set of shots come a week later, which are Flu/Rhino/Potomac Horse Fever and West Nile. The Flu/Rhino/PHF we continue to give every three months. PHF is not a long-lasting vaccine and that is why we give it frequently during warmer months of the year.

"Most horse owners will consider this more than is needed, and I suggest you check with your vet, because theories and data change every year with regard to what the horse at home, which is not exposed to other horses, might require. My vet also recommends a second West Nile shot mid to end of July. If horses are getting a specific shot for the first time, they may require a booster at a later date. Be sure to check.

"You may also notice that some horses react to certain vaccines, others do not. If you have a horse that does, make a note and be sure to mention it to your vet.

"In addition I like to have blood drawn for Lyme titers early in the spring, mid summer, and fall. A lot of people would question this, and think it an unnecessary expense. I disagree. Lyme disease is rampant here, and I treat several horses each year. Dundee was treated twice: in the summer of '03 and again in the fall of '04. The symptoms vary from a horse like Dundee, who just seems not quite himself, and a little sluggish, to lameness, exhibiting unusual behavior such as sensitivity to having a halter or bridle put on, and suddenly stopping at fences, to mention a few. Have your vet draw blood and send it to a lab for testing (this will take at least a week before you get the results) or you may want to do the newer Snap test, where results are far quicker. But remember, once a horse has had Lyme disease, it's titer will usually be higher than normal. So why not keep on top of what is happening? Don't wait for symptoms, by then your horse has probably had the disease for several weeks.

"Equine Protozoal Myeloencephalitis (EPM) is fast becoming another disease of concern in the Northeast. Horses become infected from opossum feces that have contaminated a horse's food or water supply. Use good hygiene when it comes to storing your horse's food and feed storage containers, water buckets, and tubs. Discourage scavengers. EPM attacks your horse's central nervous system and can cause devastating and lasting neurological damage. As fifty percent of all horses in the U.S. may have been exposed to this disease, a positive blood test is very common but does not necessarily mean the horse has EPM. A vaccine for EPM is available but has unknown efficacy. My veterinarian practice does not administer the vaccine unless a horse owner requests it be given.

We worm the horses every two months, starting in January

with a single dose of Ivermectrin, and for the July and November wormings we give a double dose of Strongid. There are many products on the market to choose from, so it's a good idea to read the information about them and set up an annual schedule ahead of time. I also keep a Panacur Powerpac here—it's a five-day treatment—should any of the horses come up with a more major worming problem, and sometimes they do. But you need to have a fecal sample sent out to a good lab; we use Cornell for the results, then treat accordingly.

"I am sure that some horse owners will be shaking their heads at what is not included here in our horses' care and routine, or thinking that much is done to excess. But as I have said before, I can only tell you what I do and believe is important and best for them, in this area of the country, given the wide range of weather conditions, and knowing what is expected of them."

CHAPTER SIX

Boarding

Someone who was in our barn one day noticed an empty stall and commented upon it. I happened to know she was looking for a place to board her horse, and as that is not a situation we ever get involved in, for many reasons, had a ready response. Some private barn owners may agree to an employee or a friend having their horse on the property. And if you do, it's a good idea to have a few simple rules carefully gone over before the animal comes into your barn. It's also useful to know something about the horse that will be staying with you, such as: any bad habits either when in the barn or turned out? Any health problems?—and this is one to think about if the answer is yes, and it's something like colic, as you can bet the odds are that it will happen at night, and you or your help will be dealing with it. Is the horse used to being in a paddock on its own, or with a group?—this is a good question to start with, because if not, you can have chaos on your hands, badly damaged fields, maybe even broken fences and worse, injuries. If you stick strictly to a schedule, it's a very good idea to make the person aware of this.

Many people like the idea of company, having someone else around, not minding if their daily schedule is disrupted, and a person to ride with. But before doing so, there are a few things to think about, including the liability of having both a person and their horse on your property in this age of lawsuits, or the matter of somebody coming at all times of the day, or evening if it is summer, despite previous discussions as to when they will be in your barn. Consider that if they have a trailer, it may well end up for long periods parked in your driveway, should your barn be close to the house. And think about the future—when they see you going off to hunter paces, or shows or events, and think that perhaps this might be an activity they would enjoy too—and ask to go along with you, in your trailer, if they do not have their own. This might be all well and good for a while, but wears pretty thin after a time! Consider whether you are able to take in stride going out to the barn and turning the lights off for the fifth night in a row after they have been for an evening ride, or having to tell them that leaving dirty tack hanging in your rack room, after having been asked not to—several times—is a no no. Think about reminding them to please use their own brushes on their horse, not any of yours, and not to deplete your basket of treats. Will taking their horse out at a time when your horses are done with their exercise and settled in their paddocks for the day, cause breathtaking exhibitions of galloping, bucking, spinning, shoes flying in all directions, skid marks of alarming proportions, and your horses drenched in sweat, and having to be hosed off if it's summer or toweled, Irish knits put on, and hand walked forever should it be winter? All while you are standing in tears staring at fields that will now take a miracle to restore. Sometimes, even among friends this behavior can eventually cause a strain on the relationship, and perhaps is not worth it.

Having an employee keep their own horse in your barn should be given serious thought as well. I would be more inclined to agree to this if the employee is living on the property, not several miles away, so that in the event of a problem with their horse when they are not on the farm, can end up with you or other employees having to take care of the situation, at least until they can get here, which could be awhile, especially in bad winter weather. Discuss when they will be riding their horse, which here would not be during their working hours, unless I had asked them to accompany me. I might be jumping some cross-country fences, and do not like to do that without someone with me. Or one of my old horses might need ponying and I'd ask them to do that while riding their horse. I would also impress upon them, that my horses have priority except in the case of their horse being in an emergency situation. I believe keeping an employee's horse in your barn depends enormously on your relationship with that particular employee and whether you feel they will respect your wishes. If you do not feel comfortable about the idea, don't do it, whether for a friend or an employee.

CHAPTER SEVEN

People

BARN HELP

"Some horse owners run their own barns, and that means *every* aspect of it. They do so for a variety of reasons. Economics plays the largest role, I believe. But some people just do not like the idea of others perhaps determining how their barn and horse(s) are taken care of. Or they just like to do it themselves. For many, the idea of the liability of workers on their property is one they do not wish to address, although it's a very serious one. Worker's Compensation coverage is a must once you employ anyone, as is general liability insurance (find an insurance agent who knows something about horse farms). If you are not one of the above, then the people who you hire will play a major role in your life— and they can make it a pleasure or pure hell. It is important to remember that nothing is forever, and it's also a good idea to understand that people's lives and situations change—be prepared when you have had someone working for you for some time because it is really easy to slip into that area where you believe they will stay forever!

"We have, on the whole, been extremely fortunate, and many have stayed for very long periods. Roxie Bacon came with our first two horses and she and Richard were with us for eighteen years! The day they told me that I had better sit down as they had something to tell me, and then they told me they were moving to Colorado, I thought *that's it, having our horses at home is coming to an end.* Thank God Roxie did not leave for almost a year, giving me time to collect myself and find a replacement. But again I was lucky. Libby Dowden, who had worked for me many years part-time, took over running the barn. And many others have been with us for two-, three-, and five-year stints.

"You need a *team.* People who are, if possible, going to get along. They don't have to be best buddies, but having friction between people is a nightmare, and as a friend of mine always says when she sees someone out competing and things are not going as they normally do, "something's wrong back at the barn." You need to have a pretty good idea of the kind of person you would like to have around when you decide to hire somebody, and to be upfront when you interview them. Let them know what you require of them in the job, and personally, I am comfortable letting them know what I do *not* do, such as braiding and wrapping, neither of which I do well. A positive attitude is worth a lot, and enthusiasm too. And it nearly goes without saying: reliability and responsibility. Word of mouth when looking for, and hiring help, has always worked very well for me. Of course there have been people who did not work out, and you usually know pretty quickly this will be the case once they start the job. One way of trying to resolve this is to take them on for a paid trial period, usually a week, and see how things go, from our point of view, their point of view, and how they fit into the routine of barn and horses and get along with their coworkers. Most people will go along with this, since it gives them a chance to find out if this is a job they really want.

"And yes, there have been some who did *not* work out: the young man who came to work his first morning dressed in beautiful leather, and went off for lunch never to return; the young woman who could not be bothered to clean the snow off her car's rear window, and backed into Michael's Audi—this on top of screwing up the watering system in the indoor riding ring the previous day—we are not *that* tolerant! Or another young woman, who was asked to hack out one of the horses, but never to jump him—then, a week after she had last ridden him and he was dead lame the next day, was out on another horse with me, and said, 'Oh, that's the drop I had so much trouble getting Berry to jump'— well, she was out the gates mighty fast. I usually know very quickly who will work and who will not. I like to see their résumés, but sometimes you have to go on your instincts, and your job may be their first one. I am a very 'hands on' person, and am in the barn most of the day, so anyone who works here, has to accept that!

"In the beginning we only had Roxie, and two horses, and one, then two paddocks. When we first had horses here, Michael and I only spent weekends on the farm and did a lot of trail riding. Over the years it has changed and now I have three people working full time. If necessary, we take on some part-time help during the summer. But I and my team do many other things, not just the horses and barn. We take care of the paddocks, trails and fields, maintain the cross-country fences, and the three courses used for our schooling trials (an annual event—with an enormous amount of work involved). All the stadium fences are painted at least once a year, and we hold many cross-country clinics from May through October. When I am competing, from April through October, at least one person is with me.

"If you can offer housing, which is quite often an apartment over or nearby the barn, or as we have now, a house split into two homes, next door to ours, that's a great bonus when it comes to barn check, and especially in the event of any kind of emergency. At this time, my manager, Toby Boyce, lives fifteen minutes away in her own house, Juan Cruz is next door with his family and two sheep, and Angel Miguel lives in the apartment next to him."

VETERINARIAN(S)

"Your 'vet' is a major person in your life once you have your own barn and horses at home. As with every thing else, this has changed for us over the years. The original practice we used went over to cows and small animals, the latter very lucrative. We now, and have for many, many years, used Rhinebeck Equine. And they have grown with time, to nine partners now, adding a surgeon a few years ago, and have a large new establishment, able to handle every aspect of surgery and recovery. It is only natural to gravitate to one vet more than others, and he or she becomes your primary vet, but remember that in the case of an emergency, you get who is on call, or closest to you at that particular time.

"When setting up future appointments, you can ask for the vet of your choice. It's a good idea to get to know all the partners, as there will be times when you will need someone who specializes in an area that your primary vet may not, acupuncture, for example. I find that my vets are happy to talk to me on the phone whether they are in the office or in their trucks, if I have any questions regarding our horses, and this can often prevent an unnecessary visit.

"A farm call now is $35.00 if you have called ahead to make an appointment on a certain date, or appointments that are made for the same-day care when the office opens in the mornings. But 'urgent' weekday daytime calls have an additional $35.00 fee, and 'emergency' weekday daytime calls have an additional $50.00 fee. At night, on weekends, and on holidays 'urgent' calls will have a $75.00 fee and 'emergency' calls a $100.00 fee.

"The above additional charges are for calls that cannot wait for the next regular workday, or must be seen immediately due to their life-threatening nature. My concern with these charges are that some horse owners may not have the experience to know when a call is 'urgent,' and when it can wait until the following day. Very few would have any problems understanding the 'emergency' situation. And many horse owners' budgets may not be able to handle the added costs, so they may choose not to call their vet to what may be an 'urgent' situation, but attempt to treat it themselves. If this is the case, again I would strongly suggest speaking by phone to your vet, or to any of your practice's vets, to discuss your horse's problem before treating.

"Also you should always remember that in the event of an emergency, if you are told by the vet on call that he or she cannot come for some reason, or does not feel your problem requires a visit, and you are not comfortable with this answer, always ask for the name of the backup person on call.

"I always make sure that any horse that is being seen by my vet is in the barn. Quite a few people don't, and many vets arrive to find nobody around the barn, and treat horses wherever they find them. I feel strongly that owners or their employees are responsible for having the animals on hand. And I always tell my employees if I am not here, never hesitate to call the vet if you feel it's necessary, *never* wait—it may turn out to be nothing serious, but better safe than sorry.

"These days I find there are a number of young women veterinarians joining practices, and they seem to have more patience and a quieter manner of handling horses, especially the old horses. They take their time with the animals—and with you—which is important, because if you are like me, you want to feel they have the time to discuss their findings with you, and their suggestions for treatment, should that be necessary. Don't let yourself be left watching their truck drive away from your barn, with just a written report in your hand, some of which you do not understand. Never be afraid to ask questions if there is anything that you do not feel totally clear about, especially when it comes to the cost of medications, or procedures.

"Unlike small animal veterinarians, who see their patients in a heated or air-conditioned indoor environment, equine vets very seldom do. They often work in the most frigid conditions, doing delicate procedures in badly lit areas, or in heat and humidity, amid the flies and mosquitoes. So I feel anything an owner and/or their barn help can do to make their visit run as smoothly as possible is appreciated. I doubt many horse owners in most areas of the country have any idea what it would be like to have horses in one of the more remote and less populated states, where a veterinary facility could be over a hundred miles away."

FARRIER

"Your farrier is going to be a very important person in your life from the moment a horse sets foot in the barn! Being able to get the one of your choice when you first start out may not always be easy, since the good ones have many clients and do not always want to take on new ones, and may not want to deal with a small barn. So you may have to wait awhile, and use someone else other than your first choice at the beginning.

"Blacksmiths have a reputation in the horse world for often being 'prima donnas,' not wanting to listen to the questions, let alone suggestions, of the owner. And some are reluctant to discuss hoof/shoeing related problems with your vet, feeling they can solve whatever the trouble may be without outside input. Others may leave you for days before coming to reset a lost shoe.

"We have been fortunate not to have experienced any of the above—for many years our horses have been in the hands of Tom Pavelek, his partner, Tim Jessup, and their assistant, Norm Rutledge. I always listen to what Tom has to say, especially when a new horse comes into the barn, with regard to its feet, and if changes are necessary to its shoeing, for what I require of the horse. And he and Tim are very open to any questions I may have, and there is never a problem about discussing a situation with our vet. I have never waited more than twenty-four hours to have a shoe reset. Once Dundee lost a shoe the night prior to a local event, and Tom was here before 7 a.m. the next morning, knowing that was our take-off time.

"I strongly recommend that you have your horses ready for the blacksmith's visit: hooves picked out, mud brushed off legs, and if they have been standing out in the pouring rain, take off the rainsheets—nobody wants to be dripped on for the better part of an hour. If it's cold, throw a cooler on the horse. Should you have older horses—and we do—they usually find it harder and harder to hold their legs up for any length of time while being shod, and in the case of Missouri we give him 10cc of Banamine half an hour before his turn.

"When we lose a shoe, whether in the paddock, while out hacking, or while schooling, we do our best to find it! Toby even retrieved one from the water jump one time. Things like this are appreciated; it takes less time and work to reset a found shoe, than to make up a new one; it's less costly too.

"You would be amazed how often blacksmiths, like vets, arrive at the time and date fixed, and no horse(s) in sight, no people around. So they end up bringing in the horses—or maybe they don't, in which case everyone loses. And remember, just like the vets, your farrier is going to be shoeing in the bitter winter weather, as well as the sweltering heat of summer, so make his time with your horses as easy as you can. A hot cup of coffee or tea in the winter and something icy cold in the summer is often much appreciated!

"I am sure the cost of shoeing varies in different areas of the country. But it is never cheap. I pay $135.00 for a set of new shoes, plus $20.00 for a new pair of pads. Resets are $125.00, plus $5.00 for reset pads. Borium or studs can cost between $10.00 and $25.00 per horse. In the wintertime, we put snowball pads on at a cost of $30.00 a pair, and the horses are 'sharp shod,' which simply means more borium/studs—again at $25.00 per horse. And then there are the miscellaneous costs that can appear, such as the charge for coming to reset a lost shoe—usually

$25.00. Silicon/patch work costs $25.00 if it is a small, straight-forward job. And any specialized shoe or pad will cost extra. Naturally, should you fall sometimes into the category of two new/two reset, then the charge will be slightly lower. But the bottom line is, that anyway you look at it, shoeing is a costly factor that should be carefully gone over, before owning horses, whether they are at home or not. Many people pull their horses' shoes during the winter months—and if you are one of them, that will make a difference in your annual shoeing bills."

Feed Stores/Hay/Straw, etc.

"We deal with two feed stores locally—one from which I buy our feed and the other, our shavings. Both deliver and there is a delivery charge. It's a good idea to know their delivery schedule for your area and to give them a few days' notice.

"Your 'hay man' is someone you want to always be on good terms with, because you never want to be in a situation where you find you are running low, especially in the winter months! The right hay man will tell you when he has some particularly good hay that would be of interest to you, and will keep you in mind when the summer is overly wet, and hay is going to be scarce and costly. This is another area where I have always found 'word of mouth' to be the most reliable. Know what your hay requirements are for the horses you have, what 'mix' you like, and the amount you need. This may be dictated by your storage space, but my advice is, if possible, get what you need to see you through the winter months early, as bad weather can play havoc on deliveries.

"When we first had horses here, they were all bedded on straw. I prefer it, it's warmer and cleaner. But over the years, for different reasons, we only have three horses on straw now during the winter, the rest are on shavings, and there are shavings in all the sheds from spring to fall. So I do not need to load up on straw as I once did. But I always make sure I have enough for our needs. I use wheat straw, and always hope it will be like the old days, when straw was a good length, not short and somewhat chaffy as it now seems to be."

MISCELLANEOUS PEOPLE

"Don't for one minute think that just because the following come under this heading, that they are not important. They are. You may not require some or any of their services, but over the years, and with the loss of Harold, we have. Detlef Juress took over for many years. He built our trailer barn, razed and rebuilt our 'studio barn' which is actually a two-car garage, and barn laundry. He's built all twelve run-in sheds over the years, and put in an automatic watering system for six winter paddocks. And he used to snowplow the driveway, as well as undertake other maintenance chores. Now most of this is done by Toby, Juan, and Angel, with Matt Cady doing the snowplowing. You may not have any of the outbuildings above, but if you have just one, they will need checking, servicing in some way, maintenance, repairs, you name it, they are going to need it!

"Peter Banks is another person, who comes on weekends, and takes care of some of the things we just do not have time to get to—mending fences, cleaning up the trails that require the equipment we do not have, or doing barn repairs.

"Vince, the 'tree man.' More important to Michael than me, but when it comes to 'cleaning up' the cedars in some of the paddocks, he's your man, or I am sure you can find someone just like him.

"And, of course, the person who is going to haul out your manure pile—for us it's Len Slezak. He may be willing, but the weather must cooperate, and in our case we have to haul out across one of the paddocks. He has his own equipment, backhoe and large truck.

"The person who does your fencing. If you have a small setup and can do the fencing—whatever type you decide on—that's great, because fencing is another expensive part of having horses at home.

"And never forget to have the telephone numbers of a good plumber, electrician, and major appliance person on hand.

"For many years now, Michael and I have held a dinner around Christmas for all the people who weave in and out of our barn life. The people who work with the horses: Toby, my barn manager; Juan and Juan's wife, Dolores, who helps in the house; and Angel. The blacksmiths; our primary vet, Nina Diebel, and her husband; the lady, or ladies, who keep the garden looking so lovely. Lauren, Trina, and Lesley, who used to work in the barn; Peter; Aubrey who mows; Lida, who is our cross-country trials secretary and takes care of my books; Libby Dowden, who has been a part-timer and barn manager and my trainer, and her husband, Bill. Rebecca Coffin, who coaches me with one of my horses, and her husband, Bill, to just mention a few. It's a great way to see everyone, and we hope to let them know how important their roles are. Good fences make good neighbors as the saying goes; I believe good relationships make things work!"

In case it's escaped your attention, this is a lot of people, but caring for horses is likely to call upon a lot of people, depending on how many you have and what you intend to do with them. There was a time, not so long ago, when out of sheer necessity people did a good deal of their own vet care. On the prairies, on the cattle ranges of the West, on farms and ranches in remote places, far from a town, there was no easy way to summon a vet, and very little chance he would get there before the animal died or recovered on its own, nor were there that many vets to begin with. Besides, to people eking out a precarious living from the soil, either in crops or in cattle, a vet's bill, however small it might seem to us, might be the famous "straw that breaks the camel's back."

In any case, though the vet might bring to a case his experience, judgment, and a certain knowledge of anatomy, he had no miracle cures in his black leather bag or in the back of his horse-drawn buggy. The days when the vet would be able to summon up elaborate blood testing, X rays, the full armamentarium of modern medicines and antibiotics, and sophisticated and anti-septic surgery, were many decades ahead, and left to themselves, farmers, ranchers, cowboys, and cavalrymen in the field simply applied the folk remedies they had learned, and hoped for the best.

On the other hand, hardly anybody did their own shoeing, and it is no accident that the name "Smith" is so widespread throughout the English-speaking world. Whatever England's deficiencies in the years following the Norman Conquest, an absence of smiths was apparently not among them, and when ordinary folk began to acquire a "family" name, some two or three hundred years later, many of them taken simply from their profession, "Smith" became commonplace, since there were so many of them. The local smith, with his leather apron, his forge and his anvil, and his powerful forearms, was a fixture of even the most miserable hamlet or village ("Under the spreading chestnut tree, the village smithy stands . . ."), a respected and instantly recognizable craftsman on whom everybody depended, from the squire down through all the social classes, except of course for those at the very bottom who couldn't afford to keep a horse. In the armies of the Western world, when cavalry was on the move, the farrier traveled with them, his mark of office a sharpened, polished axe, for traditionally it was also his job to put down horses which were wounded or critically lamed with a single stroke to the carotid artery. No matter how dreary and flea-bitten a Western town might be, it always contained a smith—for the ability to trim a hoof, forge a shoe, and put it on without laming the horse has always been, rightly, regarded as indispensable to the keeping of horses, and therefore, through much of history, to commerce, transportation, agriculture, and warfare.

A good smith—or farrier, as they prefer to be called, from the French verb *ferrer* (to shoe a horse)—is not only a skilled craftsman, but also somebody who has real understanding of the horse's foot, in all its complexity, as well as a feel for how to compensate and correct for problems and deformations of the hoof. The Greeks and the Romans shod their horses—therein was, in fact, the beginning of modern technology and the use of iron, and for this reason Vulcan was among the most honored of the gods—and the knowledge of how to shoe horses is an ancient art, only slightly changed by advances in modern technology and metallurgy.

The major change, in fact, is that the farrier now comes to the horse, instead of the horse being ridden or led to the blacksmith's shop. In the old days, the village blacksmith's was the place where men gathered to hear the news from travelers whose horse needed a shoe tightened or replaced, and smiths were therefore, particularly in the America colonies, likely to know how to read and have some knowledge of what was going on in the next county or beyond. They were also relatively prosperous. People might put off the purchase of a new pair of boots, but no sensible person could put off shoeing his horse when it was time to do so.

The farrier is, therefore, perhaps the last of the traditional artisanal craftsmen, in an age when most of the things that were once handmade are made by machine and mass-produced. A smith from the eleventh century might be startled by the modern farrier's truck and cell phone, but not by much else about the process. Once the farrier started to work on the horse, nothing would surprise him. The shoes are mostly pre-formed in different sizes today, instead of being made from bar iron, but trimming the horse's hoof, heating the shoe over the forge, reshaping on the anvil, and attaching it with nails, all this is done as it always was, in no way different from what would have been done in Caesar's camp, where, no doubt, the sound of the hammer and the anvil were heard throughout the day.

This is to say, of course, that the farrier is a person of some importance and the inheritor of a long tradition and an ancient craft, and should not, therefore, be treated with discourtesy or lack of respect, or as an ordinary workman on call. A really good farrier knows more about your horses' hooves than anybody— often, in fact, more than the vet. Indeed there's a saying among farriers that once a vet starts working on a horse's foot what you get is "big knife, big bill, lame horse." To this, of course, a vet would reply that he or she sees the *whole* picture of the horse's health, not just the feet, and that the blacksmith is a skilled craftsman, not a trained scientist, and there's some truth to that too.

In any event, the two people with whom you need to form a good working relationship if you're going to keep a horse at home, are the farrier and the vet, and ideally, they should know and have a certain respect for each other.

The most important thing is to find people in whom you have absolute, full confidence, because when the chips are down and there *is* a real emergency, you're going to be counting on them completely, so make this the first item on your agenda.

CHAPTER EIGHT

Feeding and Caring for the Horse

If there is one thing experience has proved it's important that horses are kept on a regular schedule for feeding, and that they will need a certain amount of time, at least an hour, after being fed to digest before they can be ridden.

The requirements of each horse in terms of feed and special supplements should be noted down and placed where it can't be missed by whoever is preparing the feed.

As for feed, Margaret's advice is as follows:

FEED

"Your choice of feed and supplements, as well as the quantity you feed will depend a great deal on several factors, including what type of horses(s) you have: brood mares and foals, horses in a serious work schedule, for example getting ready for competitions such as eventing or endurance riding or driving, hunt horses, or weekend trail riding horses, and of course the older horses. You will soon learn that there are many companies producing horse feed, some national, and others local. What you buy may depend on which of these companies your feed store deals with. Most feed stores will carry one or two different manufacturers' brands, others may be able to offer you a wider range. In my case, within a radius of a few miles there are at least three feed stores offering me a variety of choices. Do not overbuy feed in the hot weather. A good feed store will have better storage facilities than you or I may have. In hot and humid weather during the daytime, one way to keep your feed as fresh as possible, is to open the top of your feed bin and attach a box fan to the side. This will help circulate the air, at the same time keeping the flies away. When your bins are empty, and before adding new feed, clean them out. We use the small vacuum and then a damp towel.

"This is what you will find in my feed room:

"A feed and supplement list for individual horses. Feed buckets for each horse—rinsed out after each use and scrubbed with hot water once a week. (If you have several horses, you can have a different color bucket for each one, or you can put a strip of duct tape with their name on it.)

"The supplements are kept in old coffee cans, with whatever size scoop is needed, and always with a lid. That way, should one get knocked over, none is spilled. And you can keep them filled from the large container as needed. They sit on a shelf built into one section of the feed bin.

"At least two feed scoops.

"A long-handled, large spoon for mixing feed, supplements, and oil together. And should you be adding medications, whether liquid or pills, whole, cut in half, or crushed, make sure they are very well mixed, maybe add some molasses, and do check to see your horse has eaten them. In fact, I make it a rule to check out the horses' feed tubs after each feeding so we know if anything is left. It is very often a sign that things are not o.k. Should it be a small amount then it gets added to the next feeding. But in the hot weather it is a bad idea to leave any leftovers, as they attract flies and sour very quickly. They should be thrown out.

14% Pellets. (Nutrena)

12% Sweet. (Nutrena)

Steamed Crimped Oats. (Nutrena)

One of the "senior " feeds. (Nutrena)

One of the extruded "senior" feeds.
(I use Vintage Senior made by Blue Seal.)

Wheat Bran. (Nutrena)

Hay Stretchers. (Blue Seal)

Beet Pulp* shreds with molasses.
(Made by a company in California.)

---

*I know there are different opinions on how one should feed beet pulp. Here it is always soaked for at least eight hours before being fed to the horses. And as it sits around for that amount of time we keep it covered with a towel.

"I also have the following supplements, and miscellaneous stuff:

"Corn oil. Add to each feed. It can be a capful to a quarter of a cup. Older horses do well with extra oil in their feed. Keep a squirt bottle for your corn oil sitting in a coffee can. That way you avoid grain sticking to the always-oily bottle. Refill this from your large container when needed. And remember in really cold temperatures, it's best to keep your corn oil in the heated tack room.

"Garlic. We bought a bag from a Canadian distributor; it is sort of flaky and we keep it in a tightly sealed plastic bag in the refrigerator, to try and eliminate the odor. We sprinkle the garlic sparingly into feed once a day, as a tick preventative.

"Salt blocks. I keep one in each stall, either in a holder on the wall by the feed tub, or in the feed tub. Same in the run-in sheds. In hot weather and high humidity you will notice moisture around the block or dripping down the wall. It's not a big deal and can be wiped up when you clean out your feed tubs.

"Electrolytes. There is a wide range to choose from, mainly due to assorted flavors! We have apple.

"Accel. Balanced supply of essential nutrients, vitamins, minerals, and amino acids, and microbials (probiotics).

"Grand Complete. Offers a lot in one expensive bucket! Including glucosamine for joints, biotin and methionine for hoof maintenance, vitamins C and E, and yeast, to mention a few.

"Probius. I keep a jar of this, as it is wise to use when you have a horse on antibiotics. And I keep my old horse, Missouri, on a scoop each day.

"We give the horses a bran mash once a week, on Sundays, and when we get back from a competition, or when a newcomer arrives after traveling. At the end of a really nasty wet cold day, or if a horse has been treated for colic, or colic symptoms, we will wait awhile, and then more than likely give it a nice bran mash. If you are not comfortable with making this decision, discuss it first with your vet. Remove the salt block from the feed tub before giving a mash; the liquid content will cause a certain amount of melt and result in a very salty meal. Replace the salt black later or the following morning."

HAY

"We all want 'good' hay, but what is good for you or for me may not be good for others. None of us wants dusty, stalky, or, God forbid, musty, badly cured hay, of course, but what I consider necessary in a bale of hay for my horses I have at this time, may not be what is right for yours. I do not want what I call 'orchard grass' but I know plenty of people who have horses who only require this and do very well on it. I like the hay to be a good greenish color, not yellow, a mix of timothy and broome for feeding most of the year. And in the winter, I like a bale to have some alfalfa and clover. I also buy some bales of pure alfalfa, because during this time of the year I like to add a little extra to my horses' diet. Use caution when feeding alfalfa though—it is very rich. The weight of bales can vary quite a bit, and that's something to remember to ask about before delivery, as you might not want to be moving sixty-plus pound bales around. Store away from light, as your hay will bleach out, and this, together with overlong storage, will cause some loss of nutrients. When ordering, plan how much you will need. Don't have it hanging around too long. Due to unusually rainy summers in '03 and '04 hay costs have risen noticeably. Whereas I was paying between $3.50 and $5.00 for a bale of hay then, now for a nice second cutting, the price is anywhere from $5.00 to $6.50 a bale, and I know of people who are paying $7.00 to $8.50. And alfalfa is getting up to $9.00 a bale."*

GRASS

"A word of caution. It is always lovely to have plenty of grass turn-out for our horses, but when it comes along in the spring, be very careful to introduce your horse(s) to it slowly. And be especially cautious when grass is wet. I usually begin by putting a horse in a good grass area for half an hour and gradually work him up to longer periods. Colic and laminitis are both very com-

---

* These prices are based on the time of writing the book.

mon results of too much spring grass. Plus, your horses will gain weight rapidly, so if you want to get them fit and well conditioned—and to stay that way from spring on, for your trail riding, showing, eventing or whatever plans are afoot for you and your horse—watch that new spring grass intake, or you will end up with a horse that looks like a Butterball turkey!

"I think it is important to know when you buy a horse what it is being fed and how much. And at least for a period of time while it is adjusting to it's new routine and surroundings, stay with what it is used to. You may not be able to get the exact same brand, but you will be able to give the horse the same type of feed. If you want to make changes, do it over a period of time, and slowly lessen or increase the amount of grain. The same goes for supplements—ask what the horse has been used to—and make any changes you feel necessary over a period of time in accordance with the products you use. An example might be that the horse is used to one brand of joint supplement, and you may have a preference for another. I have not found any problems in switching over. But if this concerns you, I would not hesitate speak to your vet, or seek the advice of an equine nutritionist."

"There is no reason why a barn should be malodorous, encrusted with dirt and cobwebs, or an eyesore, as many are. It need not be *luxurious,* but it should always be *clean*—and neat. Horses, like the rest of us, do better in clean surroundings, so it makes sense to provide them with what they need.

"Certain luxuries make good sense: fans mounted in the right places—we use ordinary ones from K-Mart to keep the air circulating in the summer—a radio tuned to a music station to keep the horses (or at any rate the barn help) relaxed and happy. Some people have an insecticide spray system with a nozzle in each stall to keep down the insect population, which didn't work for us, but may for you, but we *do* have (and highly recommend) a fire detection system, with a sensor in the ceiling of every stall, and several more in the hay/straw storage loft. A sudden rise in temperature sounds an alarm and, more important, is connected to the local fire company, and if you've ever seen a barn fire, you'll appreciate the value of this. Fire extinguishers should also be conveniently located, instantly identifiable, and regularly serviced, with up-to-date inspection tags in accordance with the local fire codes. And everyone should know how to use them— once a fire has broken out is not the time to start wondering about how to use a fire extinguisher, or whether it's still in working condition.

"A place for everything, and everything in its place," is good advice when planning a barn. Leaving things scattered about— whether forks, rakes, anything with a pointed end, wheelbarrows, etc.—merely increases the odds that a person or a horse will trip over them, with unfortunate results. Nobody can make a barn a *totally* safe place in which to work—horses create a certain level of danger, like industrial machinery—but good planning and rigorous neatness can dramatically reduce the level of risk both to humans and animals.

A simple but effective wall of tools.

"Roxie Bacon, early on in looking after our barn, established 'a wall,' on which all cleaning implements were neatly hung in predetermined places, which is still the system we use, and has the advantage of showing instantly when something has gone missing.

"The feed room contains a wooden bar which holds some of the tools that may come in handy during a day in the barn: screwdriver, pliers, hammer, etc.

"Ours is not necessarily the best, or only, arrangement, but what matters is to develop one that works for you and stick to it. At the end of the day everything should be clean and back in place, and if something isn't, the fact is instantly visible.

"This applies—or ought to apply—to everything."

MEDICATIONS

"The tack room contains a glassed-in medicine cabinet, in which everything you need for daily care or an emergency is in place and at hand—no panicking when you suddenly need vetwrap, or Banamine, or an antibiotic ointment, or whatever.

"The medications are either kept in this cabinet, in a cupboard in the laundry room, or, if required, in the refrigerator. The way in which the medications and the cabinet are kept can be a source of easy irritation to me, and over the years, most people who have worked here have learned that very quickly. I clean the cabinet out once a week, line up the jars and bottles, labels

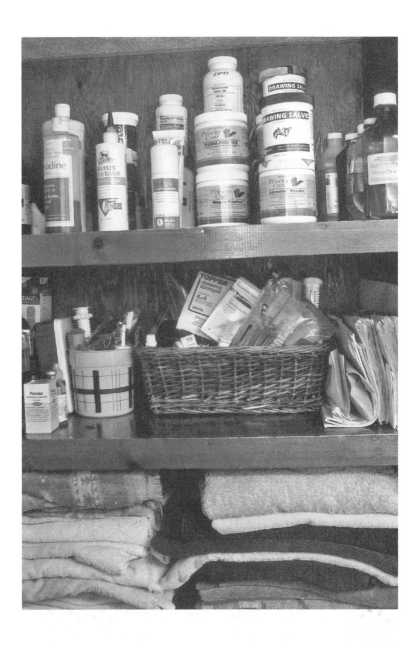

facing front, tops tightly on. I do not want to find cough syrup or hoof toughener coagulated on the sides of the bottles, nor do I want to find the molasses bottle stuck firmly to the shelf, because nobody wiped it off after use. God help the person who thrusts an arm into the cabinet to get hold of a specific thing, pushing the remainder of the stuff helter skelter, then leaving it that way. I keep towels in various sizes on the bottom shelf. It should not require a rocket scientist to keep them neatly in piles according to their size.

"There will be items in your medicine cabinet that are basic, and probably those will be in place before your horse or horses arrive at the barn. There will be things you will realize it is a good idea to have on hand as time goes by. There will be the medications that you may be using for specific horse, and there will quite likely be medications left over from treating a horse. When you can no longer read the writing on a label, throw it out. Check on expiration dates. Often your vet will exchange outdated items."

"My Basic List, 'A'"

1. Towels (assorted sizes)
2. Cotton roll
3. Sterile gauze pads (4x4)
4. Vet wrap. I buy it by the case, it is more economical. This is kept in the laundry room.

5. Dressing sponges for post-surgical wounds

6. Elastikon. Good idea to check into whether you can purchase from a local hospital supply outlet, as this item is expensive from your vet.

7. Tongue depressors

8. Bandage scissors

9. Epsom Salts. Kept in laundry room.

10. Q-tips

11. Hydrogen peroxide. Good for removing bloodstains.

12. Mineral oil

13. Baby oil

14. Vitamin E oil

15. Vaseline

16. Rubbing alcohol. Good for sterilizing thermometer after use, and the alcohol will dissolve any debris stuck to thermometer. Not recommended to clean a wound; it takes ten minutes to properly disinfect with alcohol and stings a lot.

17. Thermometer. Either a regular one—which should be attached by string to a clothespin (when using, clip pin to horse's tail), or a digital one that comes with disposable covers.

18. Dosing syringe to give medications to horses who will not eat them in their feed.

19. Probiotics. When giving any antibiotics it is important to always add a probiotic—live naturally occurring microorganisms—to your horse's feed, similar to a human eating yogurt while being on a course of antibiotics. It is available in either a powder or granule form. Suggested dosage will be on the con-

tainer, and you can always discuss it with your vet. It is important to continue use from two to seven days after the course of antibiotics has ended. I use Probius, manufactured by Microbial Products. A probiotic can be found in many tack or feed stores, or you can get one from your vet.

20. Pepto Bismal. For diarrhea. Do not use without consulting your vet. Make sure you know the correct amount, and remember it's a long way from a horse's front end to its rear, so it may take about twenty-four hours to work.

21. Electro-Plex Paste (electrolytes). Keep four to six tubes on hand, depending on number of horses. When buying note expiration date.

22. Nitrofurazone (Furacin ointment). For putting on a wound site, and for use as a sweat wrap.

23. Furall spray. I often use this after using the above, when I want a wound to dry up.

24. Ichthammol drawing salve. It is just that, a drawing ointment. Often used on sore feet. We also use it on tick bite sites.

25. Alu Shield Spray. Acts as a protective "skin" over minor wounds, especially good during fly season.

26. DMSO gel. Good to apply on swellings and heat. Wear gloves when using, as it is absorbed through the skin.

27. DSMO mixed with liquid Furacin. Especially good for wounds associated with swelling. (See above about wearing gloves.)

28. EPF-5. Keep cold in refrigerator. For reducing inflammation, swelling, sprains, or pain. Can be used as a brace after work.

29. Magna poultice. Foot abscesses.

30. Desitin. For use on scratches.

31. Betadine scrub. For cleaning wounds initially, or for infected wounds. Dilute as per instructions.

32. Betadine solution. Excellent antiseptic. Can be used alone or in a mixture as a hoof toughner.

33. Nolvasan solution. This is excellent for hot packing a wound site. And like the above, can be used for cleaning wounds. As with Betadine, it must be diluted as per instructions. And both will stain things, Betadine more so than Nolvasan.

34. Biozide Gel. Antibacterial wound dressing. For use on a more serious site than Furacin Ointment. Also good for rain rot, but use sparingly.

35. Medicated wound cream

36. Excalibur sheath cleaner

37. Swat. Clear and Medicated. Fly and mosquito deterrent around wounds, and sheath area.

38. Gnat-Away

39. Coffee grinder. The best way to grind up pills to put in feed.

40. Sunblock. For horses with light-skinned muzzles, such as Appaloosas and Paints, who easily sunburn.

41. Box of disposable rubber gloves

42. First Aid Kit for humans, and hand cream!

"Just about everything on the above list can be bought from a catalog, or at your pharmacist, local tack shop, or feed store. Several items are duplicated. This usually occurs when you buy something new before the old jar or container is quite empty. You do not always get exactly the same thing. Sometimes a variety of the above come with a prize or part of an award you may win. You may get enthusiastic when in a new tack shop and faced with a multitude of products, decide to try something different."

"My Basic List, 'B'"

"These are items I personally like to have on hand, and they come from my vet. If you are going to give intramuscular shots at home, make sure that you, or someone who works for you, knows exactly what they are doing. And be sure to have the correct size needles and syringes on hand at all times.

1. Acepromazine (tranquilizer). When using 'Ace,' knowing the size and weight of your horse is important. The dosages I use are for an average, well-built horse between fifteen and sixteen hands. For a pony, small horse, or something larger than I have, you will need to get advice from your vet. We only use Ace on a horse that has been stall bound for a period of time, due to injury, and needs to be kept quiet when first turned out, or for a new arrival being introduced to its paddock and neighboring buddies for the first time. I give 3 cc. Or if you have a horse that is bad at having its mane pulled, or when being shod, then 1 to 1.5 cc. I always keep a syringe with 3 cc of Ace in the truck glove compartment when traveling. You may never need to use it, but in the event you do, you will not want to be waiting around for a vet to come and administer. Ace should not be used on stallions because it may cause paralysis of the penis.

2. Flunixin Meglumine (Banamine*). For pain. Has anti-inflammatory and fever reducing effects. Commonly used for the relief of pain associated with colic and after surgery. A standard dose is 1 cc per 100 lbs. of body weight, with a maximum dose of 10 cc, unless otherwise directed by your vet. Do not use this product unless you have discussed beforehand with your vet. Banamine also comes in granules and paste form, but remember these will take longer to work than a shot. I always keep a syringe of 10 cc ready for use, in a labeled envelope in the medicine cabinet.

3. Phenylbutazone (Bute*). Anti-inflammatory. Comes in tablets, paste, or injectable. I always keep a bottle of pills and several paste tubes on hand. If you are giving for lameness, do not give bute in the twenty-four hours prior to a vet's examination to diagnose the source of lameness.

4. Animax. An antibacterial, antifungal steroid ointment. Used for skin problems. Avoid unnecessary and overuse, which often happens. Steroids should always be used cautiously.

5. SMZ-TPM (Sulfamethoxazole and Trimethoprim). I find this broad-spectrum antibiotic is the most frequently prescribed.

6. Doxycycline Hyclate. Antibiotic. Often used for the treatment of Lyme disease.

7. Quartermaster (penicillin). Comes is small plastic syringes. Good for using in small, but deep wounds, i.e., punctures.

---

*Both Banamine (#2) and Bute (#3) will reduce a fever, so it is important to take a horse's temperature before giving the first dose, so you don't "hide" a fever.

8. Dexamethasone (Azium* powder). Steroid. Individual packets. Most often used in cases of allergic reactions.

9. Diphenhydramine with Dexamethasone.* An antihistamine/ steroid cough syrup. Useful to have for spring/fall related allergies. Administered orally, so you will need a dosing syringe. I find it's easier to give if you stand on a mounting block, so you have the 'high ground' and have somebody else keep the horse's head up, while you dose it and then try to keep its mouth closed until it has been swallowed.

10. Isoxsuprine. It is thought to increase blood flow in the case of navicular disease and often used for chronic lameness in older horses.

11. Antibiotic eye ointment. There are many, and I have not named any specific one, as your vet will supply you with his or her choice. Used for conjunctivitis (pink eye), irritated eyes due to flies, injuries, allergies, or a blocked tear duct, for example.

12. Atropine (eye ointment). Only use as per your vet's instructions. As this will dilate the pupil, it is important to know that the horse will be sensitive to light when used, and should be kept inside or, if turned out, wear a fly mask with a 'patch' over the affected eye. (Such a patch is easy to make— I take two old fly masks and sew a piece of old towel over the left eye in one, and the right eye in the other!)

---

*Steroids like Azium (#8) and Diphenhydramine (#9) should be used only on a vet's recommendation as they are strong anti-inflammatories that have been linked to laminitis and they may inhibit your horse's immune system.

Note that you can only obtain the above medications directly from your vet, or from a catalog with a prescription from your vet. Some horse owners prefer the latter as it can be cheaper, but you must bear in mind that you may not have on hand what you want when you need it. Should you have leftover medications from previous use, again I would suggest checking both the expiration date and with your veterinarian before using them."

MISCELLANEOUS

"Annual Shots. (See Chapter Eight on Caring for the Horse.) You can also buy these from a catalog with a vet's prescription, along with necessary needles and syringes.

"Worming. I order all our worming products once a year from a catalog, making sure to ask that the expiration date is good to cover the coming year."

TACK ROOM SHELVES

"This is where I keep miscellaneous supplies like shampoos (Absorbine SuperPoo, Exhibitor's Quic Silver, and Cowboy Magic Stain Remover). Also:

1. ShowSheen. Used after bathing before a show, but never on the saddle area or on mane, as it is very slippery and you do not want your saddle sliding about, or your mane difficult to

braid. Used in tails all summer to help prevent ticks from getting a hold and climbing up.

2. Bigeloil. A general soother for sprains, strains, bruises, and stiffness. Often used for rubbing down legs after interval training or the cross-country phase at horse trials.

3. Thrush Buster. For treatment of thrush. Handy bottle which can be squirted under the pads if needed.

4. Tuff Stuff. A hoof dressing used around nail holes and coronary band in extended wet and muddy conditions.

5. Fiebings Hoof Dressing. Used on dry feet, usually during summer drought, winter ice, or packed snow.

6. UpTight Poultice. For use after a hard work out, suspensory or tendon injuries, heat or swelling.

7. Neatsfoot Oil. I use twice a year for soaking stripped tack.

8. Repel-X. A concentrated insect repellent. Dilute according to instructions. Also comes in ready to use bottle.

9. Hornet spray

10. Pine-Sol. Diluted with water and kept in a watering can during spring, summer, and fall, for sprinkling the aisle after the barn is cleaned.

11. Windex

12. Large and small clippers

13. Kool-Lube. Cooling agent to keep blades cool while clipping.

14. Blade oil. Lubricates blades while using.

15. Blade wash. (Kept in a coffee can with lid.) For cleaning blades after use.

16. Funnels. Miscellaneous sizes.

17. Flashlights. Two medium-size and one large which gives a

lot of light and can be left standing on the ground to allow you the use of both hands.

18. Assorted batteries
19. Lightbulbs
20. Leather punch
21. Braiding kit
22. Easy boot
23. Duct tape
24. Pocketknives (kept in their cases)
25. Tool box
26. Stud box
27. Large kitchen garbage bags. For trash cans in tack room and laundry room. We also keep a supply of "contractor bags," for carrying hay, and also for dirty horse laundry when we're at events.
28. Assorted Ziploc bags. For feed and treats when traveling. And other assorted uses.
29. Saran Wrap. Use over sweat before bandaging and wrapping leg.
30. Brown paper. Grocery/shopping bags or shavings bag. Cut into size needed and store; you never know when you may need them. Soak before using. Wrap over poultice before bandaging and wrapping.
31. Vacuum bags
32. Saddle soap, Lexol, and assorted sponges
33. Never Dull. For cleaning metal.
34. Gojo. Hand cleaner. Excellent for removing sap from horse's coats. And, of course, for your hands.
35. Rubber gloves"

Notice Boards

This is one of those small things that matter. We have two, and they need to be kept up to date. More important, they need to be *read*. In Margaret's words: "I have one hanging in the tack room. The most important and permanent item on it is a current, up-to-date list of necessary telephone numbers. The other bits and pieces of information come and go.

"And I have a second one on the feed room door, a black-board with things like the next shoeing date, the latest date when

shots and worming were done, when the diesel and gas tanks were last filled, when the tractors last serviced and the mower blades sharpened, the dates for my next truck and trailer inspections, and truck servicing.

"You may have other dates to add, but the blackboard is essential, and you can always erase the chalk and make changes."

TREATS

No matter how pressed she is for time, Margaret never forgets the horses' "treats." As she says, "Forget these and you are history! The best I think are the everyday favorites: apples—look for markets or fruit stands that sell 'drops', always a bargain, but seasonal. Carrots—available throughout the year, but take out of plastic bags, or they will quickly spoil. Both of these are best stored in the refrigerator until needed, as a heated tack room will hasten their demise in winter, as will the flies in the summer. Just be sure not to feed these treats to your horse without cutting the apple or breaking the carrot. Peppermints—buy in 5-lb. bags, and sugar cubes. We always buy 50-lb. bags of Purina Ovals and 20-lb. bags of Nutrisource Apple and Oat from our local feed store and keep plastic jars filled with them in the tack room. I have noticed that several of the vets carry a supply of the Ovals with them, to give a patient a treat—a good idea, as some horses very quickly catch on to the vet's arrival in the barn, and often exhibit a negative attitude in one way or another! Of course there are always the more exotic horses who just love prunes (pitted), marshmallows, pears, or bagels, to mention only a few!

"But there is a whole world of horse treats out there. In the tack shops, in the catalogs, and at the feed stores, if that's the way you want to go. You can purchase them for a special occasion, or maybe at Christmas time, when you can be assured they will come with holiday wrapping, labels, whatever! There are Mrs. Pastures Cookies for Horses, Applezz N' Oats, Carrot Crunchers, Orchard Sweets, Apple Slices, Tally Oats, and Stud Muffins, to mention only a few.

"Never forget: 'always have a treat in your pocket!'"

CHAPTER NINE

Tack

"One tends to collect a lot of tack over the years," Margaret notes, "and it is useful once in a while to go over pieces that have been around and not used for several years. I usually take anything in this category to The Rhinebeck Tack Shop and see if they can sell it for me on consignment. If not, I will try and find a home for it. I like to keep the tack I use on my horses to the very minimum. I use what is necessary for each horse, and stay away from the fads of the moment.

"For me, the most important piece of equipment is the saddle. It is certainly the most expensive. I have a personal preference for very old secondhand German saddles, Stübbens. And they must be made in Germany, not the newer ones, which are made in Switzerland. My all-purpose saddles are 'Siegfrieds' and I have two dressage saddles, one a Stübben 'Tristan' and the other an old 'County Competitor.' Years ago Michael gave me a new Swiss-made Stübben, but I was always flying off the horse when I used it, so back it went to the tack shop. Later I bought a secondhand Swiss-made saddle, but I never used it much; it was too uncomfortable, and has always been referred to since as 'the crotch buster.' In the old days you could pick up a German-made Stübben for not too much money, but you would have to spend a bit on repairs. Today they are very hard to find. In the fall, I have any saddles that need repair work, minor or major, taken care of. It takes awhile and can be quite pricey, but it's worth it.

"I have a variety of leather girths, in different lengths. Some of the following are girths I do *not* like to use: string girths, fleece-lined, or Neoprene. I always use a girth cover when riding at home—it can be thrown into the washing machine every day, but never when competing, unless required for a specific problem, such as a rub. I like to have stirrup leathers with a hole every half inch, otherwise I find myself punching more holes in them, due to the fact they stretch a lot. And apart from the leathers on each saddle, I always carry an extra one when I am traveling—in fact that, and an extra girth, are permanently in my trailer. I use nothing fancy or special in the way of stirrups, and always make sure that the stirrup pads are in good shape. It's a good idea not to let them wear down too much.

"There are many bridle manufacturers to choose from, and I personally do not have a particular favorite. I like black or dark Havana brown, with same color, padded flash caveson and browband. The latter, by the way, can come in a variety of options in design and color. I am not into different colored padding, or a lot of brass. Fashions change, and I can remember thirty years ago, when rolled bridles were the thing to have, and now they seem to be back in style. I truly believe that when getting a bridle, you have to consider the horse it is for. A Thoroughbred will need something different from a sturdy Irish sport horse, a draft cross from an Arabian. Larger buckles seem to go with the more expensive bridles, and you can pay anywhere from a low range of $50 to $100 upward to well over $400, including the reins but not the bit.

"Reins are a very personal choice: width, material, and either hooked or buckled ends—it's up to you. I prefer a wider rein to a very narrow one. You can find reins that are raised or flat rubber, laced, web, plain, or cotton webbing woven with rubber reins. Some are a lot easier to keep clean than others, and that may be a decisive point for you. I use rubber reins for everything except dressage, when I use laced reins, which in both cases match the bridle.

"Rubber reins do not last forever, the surface wears down and eventually they become smooth, defeating their purpose. It used to be cheaper to have the rubber replaced, now you might as well invest in a new pair. The cost of reins has skyrocketed in recent years. About thirty years ago, my father used to keep me supplied with rubber reins from England. Admittedly then they were orange rubber, but they were inexpensive, seemed to last a very long time, and I then sent them back to be re-rubbered for about $15, maybe less. Today you can find some reins in the region of $25 to $40 but your best buy is going to be between $60 to $90.

Some pairs can cost over $200. And as for hooked or buckled ends, I don't mind which, myself, but remember when you attach the reins to the bit, that the hooks are on the inside, the buckles on the outside.

"I have a lot of different bits, which have accumulated over the years. I never get rid of one because I think I may need it one day. I have tried so many bits, but always come back to just a few: two KK Ultra Bradoons, a KK Ultra Loose Ring, a jointed Boucher, a three-ring elevator, and a Nathe gag, which I have used on two of my event horses for cross-country and stadium. My friend Nancy Blinkhorn sent the Nathe to me from England, where they are less costly.

"One of my pet peeves with bits, is when I see a Pelham, for example, and the curb chain does not have a lip strap, or a full cheek without the leather keepers that holds the top ends of the bit in the correct position. The bit must be the right size for your horse and positioned correctly in its mouth. If you do not know a great deal about bits, and their uses, find somebody who can advise you, as it can be confusing, as there are literally dozens and dozens of bits today, many of which vary only slightly from one another, or are far more severe than you may need, or not enough bit for your horse!

"The remainder of my tack comes under the heading of 'miscellaneous.' A variety of cavessons and flash attachments, a figure eight and a drop, running martingales with rubber rein stops, and a standing martingale, both of which should always have the rubber martingale ring that keeps it from slipping once fitted correctly. Assorted breastplates. A padded surcingle. A pair of both side reins and draw reins. Several lunge lines. A pair of bit guards. A variety of synthetic fleeces, especially useful for rubs under the bridle, and many people like to use them on halters when traveling, and a packet of dark brown and black rubber keepers great for lost or broken leather ones.

CLEANING TACK

"I personally clean all the tack used each day about ninety percent of the time. And I am good at the job. It's the best and safest way to keep an eye on day-to-day wear and tear, and to make sure that each piece is kept in the best condition, rather like cleaning a firearm after use. I remember being at horse trials a few years ago, when my friend Mark Weissbecker asked me how I was doing, and I replied, 'I moved up, the person ahead of me broke a rein going cross-country.' He said, 'She should fire her groom.'

"Before starting on the job of cleaning tack, you will need a selection of sponges—some for water and some for soaping. Soap sponges, once used and squeezed dry, are kept in a colander. You need a four-pronged tack hook, to hang the tack to be cleaned—we hang ours from the ceiling and below it we have the wonderful 'saddle stand,' built for us over twenty-two years ago by Richard Bacon, which holds three saddles at a time, with a wooden area for the cleaning equipment at one end, and a flat area on the opposite end, which is cut out, six inches wide by thirteen inches long, so you can flip a saddle with the pommel slipping through the opening but the rest of the saddle is supported by the surrounding area, for cleaning the underneath. I use hot water and a medium-size sponge, squeezed well, and wipe down all the tack, having washed the bits and stirrups first. Oh, and *never* hang a girth up by the buckles on the elastic end, something I learned very early on in pony club—eventually the elastic stretches out, same thing when you put it away.

"I like to put a small amount of the hot water onto my tack sponge, a little spray of Lexol, and then rub the bar of saddle soap onto the sponge. I find it's a big mistake to put much on the seat—it will come off on your breeches in hot humid weather or when it's raining, and be with you for the remainder of the life of that particular pair of breeches.

"We keep a can of Never Dull to clean up the stirrups, buckles, nameplates, curb chains, if you use them, and any metal parts of the bits, before a show, and then a soft towel to bring them up to a good shine. But be careful not to get any cleaner on the mouthpiece of the bits. And if you do, wash them well.

"A tip from Roxie Bacon when she first came to run the barn—keep a large nail alongside your saddle soap, and use it to keep your leather holes cleaned out. I have found that some people who have worked in the barn, always seem to forget that rubber reins need a good wiping off. A small brush dipped in hot water cleans them best.

"If your tack gets wet, clean it, but let it sit out uncovered for at least twenty-four hours. We always 'strip' all the tack once a year, usually at the end of the year, taking it apart piece by piece, treating it with Neatsfoot oil and allowing it to lie on towels overnight. This includes tack that is not in current use, but put away in tack trunks, wrapped up in old pillow cases.

"During the hot and humid summer months, saddles and bridles that are not used regularly will often become mildewy, so checking each week is a good idea. And don't forget your leather halters, one only tends to remember them during use in the show season, but they need cleaning once a month too! My spurs are cleaned as used. Also, when I remember, all the whips are wiped over with the soap sponge.

"On the subject of saddle pads, I believe this is either a personal choice, or dictated by the special requirements for a certain horse. There are so many saddle pads out there today, one could go crazy deciding what to have. I like the PolyPads, the single thickness, (they come in three thicknesses) and a variety of colors. You can also special order most colors with contrasting trim, and I am sure whatever else you might like. Very important: they stay in place; there is nothing worse than having a pad that slips. They wash well in cold water, but do not put them in the dryer, as I find they eventually tend to get lumpy (and then you have more pet bedding than you will ever need in a lifetime). They will dry quickly in the spring/summer/early fall, by just being hung over a gate—but they will fade. At other times of the year, I hang them up in our heated tack room, but they do take sometime to dry thoroughly.

"I keep tack in regular use—bridles, girths, breastplates, martingales, extra reins, etc.—hanging on each horse's individual bridle bracket, with its name above; and saddles are covered with a washable cover, each on a separate rack, if possible."

CHAPTER TEN

Horse Clothing

"Over the many years, I have seen most forms of horse clothing take giant steps forward. It used to be that it was all one could do to even lift a heavy turn-out or stable blanket. And once they got wet—and they did—forget it. Then, suddenly, rather like ski jackets, horse blankets took a miraculous leap into the world of space-age materials, along with a wider and wider choice of colors, including checks, plaids, custom colors, with contrasting piping, if that is what you wanted. They could be quilted, and offered a choice of high cut necks, tail flaps, shoulder gussets, adjustable leg straps, different layers of poly-fill or fiberfill linings. And first, water resistant, which I found never to last long, nor respond to spraying with the recommended product before using after cleaning. And then, waterproof! I have tried them all, at one time or another. Also you seemed to need years ago, so many different weights, the light, medium, and heavy weight turnout, the liner to go under the stable blanket with stable sheet on top. And I am just talking basic stuff. We have not even ventured into other types of horse clothing.

"The first thing you must do is make sure you know the correct size that your horse or horses will need. If I am at all in doubt, I err on the side of larger. Then it's going to be very much your personal choice; economics will play a role, as it does when buying for your horse. These items can be pricey, even before you get into special colors, maybe your initials, your horse's name, farm name. So take your time, shop around, look in the many catalogs, especially when it is sale time, think ahead, try to buy your winter needs in the spring, when you can often get a good price cut.

"I have learned over the years that I do not need nearly as many pieces of clothing per horse as I once did. I reached this conclusion once I bought my first Rambos and Rhinos. I have rainsheets and medium and heavyweight blankets for each horse. On the nights the horses are in the barn, if it's cold, they keep their medium or heavyweights on, and we put a stable sheet over the top. I have not used a conventional stable blanket for years. Should the weather become frigid, we then add a stable blanket, which are now lightweight, but very warm. Never overblanket, it is unhealthy for your horse to be hot and sweaty. And regularly take a stiff brush and clean off both outside and inside of your blankets. Should you get a warm day, throw them over a gate or fence to air out.

"My rainsheets get the most use, as we always keep them over whatever is added as the temperatures drop. Periodically, when they get very muddy, they are hosed off and hung in the tack room overnight to dry, likewise when the horses come in for the night after a day out in the rain. My stable sheets get laundered at least twice a month, really depending on the amount of nights the horses are in.

"Never, never leave any blankets, sheets, etc., on a horse without removing them at least once a day. It happens—I have heard of people who have laid off horses for the winter for one reason or another, who, if the horse comes in at night, may pull off just the top layer and throw on a stable sheet, or if the horse is out twenty fours hours a day, just leave him in what he is wearing. I have driven by horses turned out for the winter, with their clothing hanging half-off, or slipped under their bellies. I have to believe that, in these cases, checking, and less likely, any grooming is not high on the care list. A lot can go on under a continually-worn blanket or sheet, and it will not be good.

"The only other horsewear items I have are several coolers for everyday use—and some really nice ones I have won at events— a couple of quarter sheets, for using when exercising in really cold weather, two Irish knits, and fly masks. The fly masks, whatever the manufacturers' blurb says, never make it through a season! So in the late winter, when there are sales, I stock up on a dozen.

"You can go absolutely crazy in the area of horse clothing. In addition to what I have mentioned above, you can buy dress sheets, stretch dress sheets, sheets complete with hoods, mesh flysheets with or without neck covers, or summer sheets that will protect your horse's coat from sun damage. A whole line of Lycra 'Jammies,' 'Sleazy,' or 'Stretchies' in eye-catching designs and colors, can be used for a number of purposes, from training the mane to lie flat, to keeping a horse clean after a bath before a show, or for added warmth. And let's not forget tail socks!

"But whatever you have, most of it will be washed at home, or, if not, sent out to professional cleaners, especially all the heavy winter stuff in the spring. There are many companies which now take care of the bigger pieces that need special handling, and also take care of repairs. The rest of your horse clothing can be handled at home, but *do* read the manufacturers' label before washing and putting in the dryer. And remember—Irish knits are famous for shrinking!"

BOOTS, WRAPS, AND BANDAGES

"One could write a small book on the above.

Bell boots. I use heavy-duty, double locking Velcro bell boots. I buy one pair at a time, usually in black or dark blue. But you will be faced with a huge variety of choice. Pull-on bells are nail breakers for most of us! Ribbed, fleece-lined, 'quick wrap,' 'no turn,' and 'petal' bells, to mention a few, are available in quite a selection of colors, even sparkly ones. A pair of straight-forward bell boots, nothing fancy, can start at around $16 to $20 a pair. But watch for sales, as with everything in the boots, wraps, and bandages departments, you can get some excellent buys.

Galloping boots. I use all-purpose galloping boots; you buy them in pairs, with reverse grip Velcro straps. The front set will be shorter than the hind pair, three velcro straps on the front, four on the hind set. Make sure they are correctly positioned when putting them on. When I school my water jump at home, and if there is water on a cross-country course, we put two strips of duct tape around each boot to help hold it in place. Do not use polo wraps when schooling water, once wet they will seldom stay in place. Galloping boots can also be called splint boots and can come in a mind-boggling array of colors, often made out of neoprene with a padded leather overlay. The can be fleece lined, or have soft orthopedic foam lining. There are even leather ones made in Italy with brass buckles, but I doubt these could just be popped into the washing machine like most of the others. And I have just scratched the surface here! Your cost can be from around $25 a pair to $150 a pair. Some horses' legs become irritated by the neoprene, especially when they get sweaty and or wet. If this is the case, switch to another type.

Shipping wraps and bandages. I like the simple cotton quilted bandages with polo wraps or barelegged, but do always use bells all-round. I used to have the shipping boots that are shaped to come up over the knees and hocks, made by various companies and out of a wide selection of materials. But as the weather is usually warm, or downright hot, when I am traveling, I felt it was just something heavier than the horse needed, and they all had a tendency to slip down. A word about any wraps: once the Velcro gets old, but you still feel you can get some life out of them, run a strip of duct tape around the wrap over the velcro strap; you do not want a wrap unwinding while you are riding.

Standing wraps and cotton quilted bandages. Always have a least one set, better two, on hand. They are washable and reversible, will reduce the cost of bandaging, and are good for many things like stocking up, transportation, and limb support in injured and non-injured legs. (Do not forget when you wrap the injured leg to wrap the non-injured leg as well. This gives the horse support on the sound limb, as it will likely put more weight on it, in an attempt to lessen the discomfort in the injured leg.)

It is important that the person wrapping knows what they are doing. If you have a new person who is unfamiliar with this procedure, make sure you show them the correct way, and I would suggest you watch them practice a few times on a sound horse before handling an injury. Legs must be wrapped front to back, snug around the front across the shin, but not pulled tight around the tendons at the back of the leg; damage can be caused by doing so. Wrapping legs correctly is a real skill.

I am personally very poor at wrapping, but am fortunate to have people here who are excellent. If you do not feel comfortable when wrapping, and you're on your own, practice with skilled supervision until you get better. Routine bandaging can be learned.

CHAPTER ELEVEN

Equipment

Until fairly recently in man's long relationship with the horse, the chief thing a human being needed was a good strong back. Almost everything to do with keeping horses required a substantial degree of physical labor, and to some degree that still remains true. We live in an age when we can send robot missions to Mars, but a horse's stall is still cleaned out pretty much the way it was in medieval times, or much earlier, with a shovel, a pitchfork, and a wheelbarrow, and bales of hay are moved, in most barns, by picking them up.

Mechanization (and plumbing) have relieved most horse keepers of at least *some* of the physical strain inherent in keeping horses, but the bottom line, as anybody knows who has done it, is that it's hard work. That is not necessarily a terrible thing—we have known quite a fair number of people who claim to get a lot of satisfaction out of mucking stalls, or grooming a horse which has just rolled in thick mud, and it may be so, but generally speaking, anything you can do to make the task easier, more efficient, and less time-consuming is probably a plus, for most people.

When we began keeping horses at home, we started off with a minimum of mechanical equipment. Over the years, we acquired an increasing number of machines, many of which were interesting antiques which Richard Bacon bought for us at bargain prices, and which—since he is one of those men who can repair just about everything—he could nearly always manage to start. That is not to say that *we* could. One of the minor annoyances of life was laboring fruitlessly for hours to start—say, an old tractor, built before the Second World War—only to have Richard show up at the end of the day and start it at the first try. For years we had a tractor which looked like something that belonged in the Smithsonian Institution and which only Richard could put in reverse, no matter how many times he showed us the particular combination of sheer physical brawn and gentle "feel" for the gears and clutch that were needed to do the trick.

In this area, you are on your own, and much depends on what you can afford to spend and whether you or your "significant other" is mechanically inclined. There are certainly plenty of bargains out there, in every barnyard and used farm machinery store, and since most agricultural machinery was designed to last forever, a lot of it can still be made to work.

Our own experience has been, in general, that new is not only better, safer, and more efficient, but in the end likely to prove a good deal cheaper in the long run, since it's easier to repair and spare parts are available. When something goes wrong, you don't want the guy who is supposed to be repairing it pushing his hat back on his head and saying, in tones of awe, "Dang, I haven't seen one of these in years!"

In any event, we list below what we now own, some of it old, some of it brand-spanking-new. Neither of us would suggest you need everything on this list—but everything on it has proved useful to us over the years, and some things, like the "Gator," have in fact proved so useful that it's hard to imagine how we ever did without them in the first place.

By the way, no matter how much machinery you acquire, a good strong back will still be a great asset in looking after horses.

MACHINERY AND EQUIPMENT

"Twenty-five years ago we did not have any equipment," Margaret recalls. "Now I am not talking about *barn* equipment, but rather things like tractors, you know, the big stuff. Harold Roe had everything one would ever need, and did not like to hear any talk of us buying anything. 'Never fear, Roe is here' was his greeting, and when Richard suggested we get an old Ford tractor, and I mean really old, almost older than me, Harold was very glum. He had come to terms reluctantly with our owning a four-wheeler, but when we bought a tiny mower to pull behind it, he was not at all happy at the sight of me, in my early mowing days, trailing far behind him. He would shake his head when he swung about and passed me by on his big tractor. Harold took care of everything: the lawns around the house, mowing in the summer, and vacuuming up the leaves in the fall before winter set in. He topped the paddocks when he thought they needed doing—we did not have many then—weedwacked when he had the time, fixed the broken fences, and dragged the paddocks. But what he loved best was being out on the trails and 'wacking back' as he would say. There were a few hunt trails crossing the land, but Harold opened up more and more trails as time went by, and they all needed mowing, needed the bushes trimmed. He cleared this, he cleared that. Later on, when we started to hold our cross-country schooling trials, he built many of the fences. And whenever I saw something on course at an event where I had recently been, Harold and I would get in the Porsche, he sitting white knuckled and stiff as if in some alien spacecraft, and we'd go and take a look so he could build one like it.

"Then, Harold died, late one afternoon in the barn, and caring for all the things he had done, became a part of my life. Oh, I did not take on the lawns, and we did try other people around the paddocks and trails, but it was never the same. I did my best with the old blue Ford tractor, but hated it, as well as the much larger International, which came a year or so after Harold's death and was a nightmare. So one day I said to Michael, 'I'm going to call the Albrecht brothers' (from whom the old Ford had been purchased), 'and see if they want to buy it back and the other tractor along with it. We're going to buy a new tractor.'

" 'Well, it's worth a try I guess,' he said, without great enthusiasm.

"I called, they were very interested, they were over within an hour, and I sold them the two tractors, and the old bush-hog and sickle bar as well, then bought a new Kubota.

"Before buying any kind of equipment, new or used, you should give some serious thought to whether you want to take care of your property yourself, or, hire someone with the necessary equipment, to do what you need. We hire certain stuff by the day, when needed, such as a stump grinder, or a backhoe.

"Everyone has a different idea of how they want their place kept. A lot depends on how much time you have to allot in your day, or week, and much depends upon your budget. If you have one horse, and it's no big deal handling things on your own, and you don't mind doing it, that's great. But it is not great if you do *not* like doing it, or do not have the time, since then it becomes just another chore. As for me, I *like* mowing, in fact I find it very therapeutic."

"At this time we have the following equipment:

Kubota Tractor, model #B2910	These four pieces of equipment I group together as the mower, brush hog, and forklift are only used with this tractor. We "lengthen" the capacity of the forklift by tying two fence rails with strong wire to each of the forks. Works very well for moving wider stuff. And make sure you have the correct weights on the front end of both tractors. This is a safety factor to maintain the tractor's balance.
Woods Five-foot Finished Mower	
Woods Five-foot Brush Hog	
Small Forklift	

Kubota Tractor, model #B2100	This comes with a 4' wide Mid Mount Mower. Good for mowing paddocks, smaller areas, etc., but I often take it out on the larger fields.
John Deere Gator	All-purpose vehicle. Great for mucking the run-in sheds.
Polaris Four-Wheeler	All-purpose vehicle, especially good for dragging. Ours comes with a blade for moving snow up to a certain depth, and it is advisable to have chains on the tires at that time of year, but don't count on it for any major form of snow removal. Ours has a winch, very useful in a variety of ways, especially when something gets stuck in the mud!
Terrapro (very old)	Second four-wheeler, sixteen years old, and only used for dragging the indoor ring, it is kept in the arena, covered with a tarp—horses take no notice of it whatsoever. Was once our only piece of equipment and we did everything with it, even mowed big fields. It took days!
Cart	Small, all-purpose, can be hitched to either tractor.
"Echo" Leaf Blower	Replaces a broom in outside areas around the barn and manure pile, and helps take care of clearing fall leaves. We provide ear and eye protection when using it.

"Echo" Weed Eater	Used solely for clearing weeds and trimming, in our case around fence lines, run-in sheds, outbuildings, as well as barn, and stadium and cross country fences. Again ear and eye protection should be worn at all times when in use.
Twenty-two-inch "Excalibur" Hedge Trimmer	For the hedge trimmer, leaf blower, and weed eater, you will need to use a special mix of one gallon regular gas with one packet of oil mix.
Snowblowers: • A small Honda HS50 • A large Ariens 1336	One of the essential pieces of equipment in the Northeast.
Drags (two)	One kept in a corner of arena, behind a gate. Dangerous if left exposed. The other, used for dragging paddocks, paths, trails if needed. Some people weigh them down with a good size log, or some cinder blocks, but a log(s) is easier to tie down.
Miscellaneous	A collection of posthole digger, shovels, snow shovels, ice picks, heavy-duty rake, crowbar, tamp, pick axe, chainsaw, bow saw, etc., pretty much depending on the climate where you live."

"With any equipment, new or old, care and maintenance is of the utmost importance. The tractors and mowers are cleaned off after every use; we use a blower first and then hose them off. We keep them greased regularly, Toby or Juan check the oil and filters periodically and change them when needed, and they also get a yearly 'checkup.' If possible, we keep them inside, especially during the winter.

"Any machinery, large or small, should only be used by people who know what they are doing. Accidents can happen very quickly, often with disastrous results. And I believe children should be kept well away from all equipment. These are *not* toys.

"Always keep a half dozen fence posts and at least a dozen rails on hand. When your supply gets low remember to pick up more as you do not want to be in a position of finding a broken rail first thing in the morning, or when horses are being checked in the evening once they are turned out for the night, coming upon the same situation—needing a rail and having none you can lay your hands on."

CHAPTER TWELVE

Care for the Aging Horse

Margaret writes: "There have been so many excellent books and articles written on the above subject by experts, and I certainly do not claim to have any special knowledge except that which I have obtained by having several of my horses grow old, alongside me.

"'Old age' comes to different horses at different times. But, usually by their midtwenties, you are certainly going to notice changes. Two of my horses that I evented, made the decision when coming back into work in the spring of their seventeenth year, that jumping was no longer for them. And x rays proved they were right. Nebraska happily and comfortably went on competing until she was coming up on twenty. Berry Fox made a comeback at twenty! Missouri has been with me for a quarter of a century, until nearly his thirtieth birthday.

"I believe you treat aging horses as you do aging people. Keep them in the routine, keep them involved, don't leave them out of the loop just because they are getting older. My older horses are on exactly the same routine as the others, every day. They get their shots, are wormed, and shod as they always have been. Exercise is very important. It does not have to be for more than twenty minutes to half an hour, but I get them out five days out of seven, minimum. I usually ride Berry and pony Missouri. Once the grass has gone, then Missouri just follows, and the more horses on the ride, the better he likes it, but he has to be in control, in the lead. Of course the two old horses only walk, and are stiff when they start out, but like you or me, they loosen up a bit as they progress. Once in a while, something will produce a spurt of activity, but I try and keep any extra found energy down to a minimum; they are generally sore later if they have put in a few small bucks, or decided to try a canter. And that is why, when there is plenty of grass, I keep Missouri on a leadline. Otherwise he will stop and eat, and not follow, until I have ridden far enough away for him to feel he must trot or canter to catch up.

"One of the most important things to be mindful of is colic. When I was a small child, I would often hear adults referring to pneumonia as "the old person's friend," a precursor to death, and I think of colic in that way with regard to old horses. Many years ago I lost an old horse to colic, and it was very fast. So it has always been something that I bear in mind, mentally noting subtle, or not so subtle, changes, when they occur, and alerting my barn help to always be on their toes regarding any out of the ordinary behavior, especially in a horse with a history of colic. With Missouri, the first sign is the flaring of the nostrils, and sometimes that's all it is, and it passes. Other times that leads to labored breathing, a noted tenderness in the area of his flanks, when if touched, he will move away and make an attempt to kick out, which he is really too old to do now. He will start to paw the ground, and attempt to go down, which he cannot do any longer. We have learned, Toby and I, when an attack merits calling the vet, and then he is usually given a rectal, tubed with mineral oil and given 10cc iv[*] of Banamine. But if the attack is mild, we administer the 10cc of Banamine, but im[†] and keep a close eye on him over the next few hours. I keep Missouri on a daily scoop of Strongid Cx2 continuous wormer and have for many years, as another hopeful preventative against an attack.

"An old horse's eating habits tend to change, so keep an eye open for this. There are many feeds on the market now for the older horse, softer, easier to chew and digest. When you think it is time to switch him to one of these feeds, do it gradually. It may also take awhile to find out which they prefer.

"If keeping weight on becomes a problem, feed more frequent meals, with as much as a quarter, to half a cup, of corn oil mixed in. I have one old horse who is fed a mash/mix at night; it's his largest meal of the day, and as he has all night to eat it, he always does. We put the supplements in this meal.

"Have good nutritious hay—I like to have some bales of

*Intravenous
†Intramuscular

alfalfa on hand, and feed a flake a day. To ensure a good intake of fluids, add electrolytes to your horse's feed. (Usually done only in the hot weather, but I do this all year round.) Many older horses urinate more frequently, which is often—and correctly—associated with one or more of the conditions that accompany the aging process. Keep your vet informed of any changes that concern you; make sure that teeth are checked at least twice a year—they can often be the cause of older horses going off their feed as they lose their teeth.

"Make sure the treats you give them are cut up, it's not so easy to bite into a whole apple any more, and dangerous should they get something large in their mouths, that they cannot chew, and choke. As horses get older and arthritic, it becomes more painful for some of them to hold their legs up for any length of time, so I give, as recommended by my vet, a shot of 10 cc of Banamine half an hour before it is their turn to be shod, which is helpful.

"If they grow good coats in the wintertime, don't over-blanket, some horses tend to sweat more as they age. And you will often find that the 'clothing' they had several years ago, just doesn't fit them quite the same, their shape has changed, so for them to be comfortable, you may need to get something new. If your horse has one of the medical conditions that go along with old age, such as Cushing's disease, they tend to grow thicker, wavy coats, (among other symptoms), and a partial clip often makes them more comfortable. I keep them out twenty-four hours a day as often as I can in decent winter weather, because confining them to a stall for many hours overnight, can increase stiffness. If they are in, I always open their top doors, as older horses often tend to develop respiratory problems they never had as youngsters.

"Be alert to the older horse who, when it lies down, has a problem trying to get back up, or who, after rolling in deep, or ice-covered snow, fails to get purchase to regain its footing, or having made several attempts, no longer has the strength it requires. Most get back on their feet with encouragement and the help of a couple of people, but if you fail to get the horse up, call your vet.

"Don't be alarmed in the physical changes you will see. All older horses, with a few exceptions, will start to drop in their backs; they won't be in such good flesh as they used to be; you will notice thickening of some of the joints, maybe an increase in irritability, and a general slowing down. You just have to have more patience. After all, they have paid their dues, they owe you nothing at this point. I am just happy to see my older horses here day after day."

Michael adds: "Here's the good news. Young or old, horses are resilient creatures. During the Crusades, it was not considered abnormal for a knight to ride his horse half way across Europe, then ship it from an Italian or Balkan port to the Near East—the horses packed in like so many sardines in small, open boats.

"The conditions under which horses were shipped across the Atlantic three centuries later by the Spanish *conquistadores* (standing crammed into narrow, improvised stalls, without ventilation or drainage, below decks in the stifling heat for months on end) did not prevent many of the horses from arriving alive—indeed it is from them that America's "native" horse population descends.

"Even in the eighteenth and nineteenth centuries, the conditions under which horses crossed the Atlantic, or were shipped from England to India when cavalry regiments were moved, would seem to us unthinkable. Of course, to be truthful, a great many of the horses died (hence the name "The Horse Latitudes" for that part of the South Atlantic where heat and contrary winds made it necessary to throw the corpses of many horses overboard), but to be realistic, the conditions under which horses were shipped were not significantly worse than that of human travelers or ship's crews, in an age of foul water, rotten rations, and constant exposure to disease—indeed, in some cases, the horses' conditions may have been better, since a cavalry mount was more valuable than a sailor or, for that matter, a cavalry trooper. Still, old or young, any notion of the horse as a delicate creature in need of constant medical care and attention does not correspond to the reality of life for horses until quite recently in history.

"They're survivors!"

CHAPTER THIRTEEN

Winter Weather, and How to Deal with It

Paying attention to the weather is something you have to accept as an important factor of running your own barn—the Weather Channel is no longer something you can ignore, at the price of getting your good shoes wet or having to buy an umbrella from a street vendor. Good or bad, the weather report is not only vital information, for today, tomorrow, or the week ahead, but is going to exert a real control over your life. A week of heavy rains and thunderstorms means you have to think of drying off the horses' rain sheets (Where do you hang them, how do you dry them, what do you do with the horses while you dry them?), keeping the horses in fields where they have some protection, making sure the water doesn't back up into the barn (Has anybody seen the submersible pump?), watching out for pulled shoes and the early signs of thrush, and making sure that the bowls of the automatic water feeders outside (if you have them) don't fill up and overflow into the mechanism. . . . And so on.

It is at periods like this when it could just possibly occur to you that having a swimming pool, rather than a barn and horses, might not have been such a bad idea after all, or that even gardening, however vigorously pursued, may be a lot easier than horse keeping.

Margaret's concern for the weather is bred into her. She remembers her childhood. "Not a morning went by when at some point during breakfast my father wouldn't lower his newspaper, look at me, and say one of the following—or some variation thereof: 'I should think the footing must have been firm this morning'. . . . 'The going hard, was it?'. . . 'Very heavy out there today?'. . . And when I was a young child, 'Bloody deep, I hope you're not galloping that little bugger of a pony over fences, he'll have windgalls the size of balloons.' All of course referred to the daily conditions of the ground when I had been out riding earlier. He never waited for an answer, just raised his paper, and went back to his tea and toast."

It's something you have to think of all the time, if you're keeping horses. Before you know it, it's blazing hot, with the grass dying off, and the horses stamping their feet on ground like concrete because of the flies, when the temperature continues to hover in the humid nineties while flash floods and overflowing ponds cut gullies the length and depth of a bus through the forecourt of our old upper annex, drench the sodden pad-docks, and tear up culverts and dump them yards (or miles) away downstream.

Mother Nature is in her wet phase, practicing to be a mer-maid, it seems, and for horse owners that spells mud, and also grass growing quicker than you can mow it. It also means, in our part of the country, a burgeoning of the insect population, and that means meticulous grooming to look for ticks, plus careful cleaning of tubs and buckets, which have to be kept off the ground when not in use, usually on a fence post, and an effort to remove standing pools of water, where mosquitoes breed. . . .

In short, it means a lot of work and forethought, and some-body in charge, and that somebody is *you,* whether you're doing it yourself or trying to ensure that other people do it the way you want them to.

Every season brings its own pleasures—and its own prob-lems, of course. Where we live, spring and autumn are glorious; summer can (as we have just read) be treacherous, and winter is all too often a severe trial. The Hudson Valley has its charms, but bad weather streams toward us from Buffalo and, farther north, Canada, freezing fingers and pipes, catching the unwary without snow tires by surprise, and making horse care something of an ordeal.

As Margaret puts it, "If you are riding your horse(s) out in the snow, a few inches of powder is great fun, but use caution when it becomes deeper than six inches, or once it becomes packed. It can be tough going, especially for the older and unfit horse.

I always ride a younger horse to 'break' a trail through the snow, then take out the older ones once there is a path for them. Be careful of riding in ice covered snow—riding through a very thin coating is OK, although I recommend wrapping your horse's legs if you do. A serious crust can cause ice cuts. In slippery winter footing it's a good idea to make sure your horse is taking small strides, and that you have both hands on the reins and are not riding 'on the buckle.' In slippery winter footing, never ride your horse horizontally along a slope, his legs can slip sideways under him, and you could both have a nasty fall. We have experienced this; luckily the two of us and our horses were fine, just shaken up. Take a vertical path, the worst that can happen is that your horse may slip down on its hind end. Keep in mind where there are areas of ice, because if you don't and you have had a few inches of snow, the footing can be treacherous."

Needless to say, a forecast of heavy snow, winter storms, a bad "Nor'easter" with high winds, ice, and sub-zero temperatures, presents a whole different set of problems and dangers, all of them very familiar to those readers who live in the Northeast and the Midwest, such as digging a path out to the manure pile after a night of snow, or worrying about getting the accumulation of snow off the barn roof somehow before it collapses.

"Living in the Northeast," Margaret says, "can be extremely tough during the winter, especially when we get snow storm after snow storm, or have a sheet of ice covering the ground from mid November on. So, my first piece of advice is make sure that you have lined up someone, well ahead of time, who will take care of your major snowplowing. That would be the driveway from the road to your house, barn, and other buildings you need access to. (Including housing that your barn help may occupy if adjacent or nearby.) Otherwise employees may arrive, only to find they cannot get off the road and onto your property.

"Then prepare yourselves, the horses, and what you will need around the barn. The right clothes and waterproof footwear, and suggest to your help that they bring extra gloves, socks, and even boots with them, in the event they get wet when working in the snow. I keep a supply of 'handwarmers' in the tack room.

"Consult with your farrier to have your horses sharp shod and snowball pads put on, ahead of bad weather.

"Check to see you have sufficient grain and shavings on hand, as deliveries maybe delayed.

"Make sure you have a supply of heating tape, and for water tubs that we use which are not automatic, we have electric heating coils.

"Don't wait until the first 'winter storm watch' announcement to start looking for stuff put away the previous spring. Get a supply of Magic Melt for use on solid surfaces, but not on snowblown paddock paths, it's far too expensive for that. We usually have a yard of 60/40 mix of sand and rock salt, kept under some kind of roof if possible. If not, cover with a tarp. Have barrels filled with the mix and placed in strategic spots, where you know there will be some traffic.

"Check any machinery that you will be using before the storm hits. Gas up the snowblower, if you have one—in our case the Polaris four-wheeler, with the small snow blade on the front. Get out the snowshovels and that handy ice-breaker ahead of time.

"The first thing done in the morning, following or during a storm, is to feed the horses. Then we start the primary clearing—a path out of the barn to the paddocks, and the manure pile. Shovel behind gates, so they can be opened wide enough to get a horse through without catching its sides. Shovel a path between the tack room and laundry room. Later, once you have caught your breath, snowblow paths from the paddock gates to the run-ins, and to the water source, so the horses at least have clear access to both, and are not floundering through deep snow and drifts. Be aware of wind direction, as you do not want your run-in sheds full of snow for longer than can be helped.

"Some people like to keep halters on their horses during extremely bad weather, making it easier to catch them, should they start running or just acting plain stupid for some reason or another. Then, once you are done with your normal routine, and if there is any time left over, there is always lots more shoveling and it's a good idea to keep an eye on any badly iced areas in your paddocks. We usually try and get some sand/salt mix out onto them for traction. Cleaning out the run-ins can still be done with the Gator, or similar vehicle, if that is what you have, but you want to drive it slowly and carefully.

"For the indoor arena we keep a dozen bags of calcium chloride flakes in the event we have a problem with the overhead watering system due to freezing conditions. When you know you have a period ahead when you will not be able to water, you can use calcium chloride to keep your dust down to a minimum, adding a few bags at a time, as necessary. Just remember, once you water, you will defeat the purpose of the flakes.

"And when the temperatures are very low due to wind chills, it's just too uncomfortable to be using anything other than a wheelbarrow, bringing it back to its full glory, and one has to plod along the cleared path, taking twice the time, if not longer. Make sure nobody stays outside for too long at one time in extremely low temperatures. Michael, when he is here, or me if he is not, makes sure that everyone has a hot coffee, tea, or chocolate midmorning and comes into the warmth of the tack room for a break."

CHAPTER FOURTEEN

A Day in the Life

A lot of time has gone by since we first set up "horse keeping," and amazed ourselves (and many of those who knew us) by bringing our two horses over to the house and putting them in our own barn. Arrangements which once seemed temporary have become permanent; improvisations which we were certain we'd change, fix, improve, or discard one day have become second-nature to us, so we can't even imagine changing them now, and in some areas additions have been made which probably ought to have been done right back at the beginning.

Some of the change has to do with scale, of course. Nobody could have predicted twenty-five years ago that Margaret would be competing regularly, or that we would have our own cross-country-course (complete with a water jump), or holding cross-country competitions and clinics on our land, or that our life would eventually involve the ownership of as many as six horses.

Of course, not all of this directly affects the barn—it's simply part of the process of expansion that tends to come over people when they start keeping horses, and develop a *purpose* for them, whether it's barrel racing or show jumping or combined training. You build up a bewildering amount of tack and equipment— filling what once seemed like an infinite amount of storage space to the breaking point—and a large number of machines, some of which you'd never imagined you'd ever own, all of them needing servicing, cleaning, and the occasional repair.

As we write this, the combination of weeks of heavy rain followed by intense heat and humidity has naturally brought the insect population out in swarms—just at the moment it's deer fly season, and no matter what you spray on the horses, they suffer from endless bites, some of which make them break out in big bumps—not to speak of the usual plague of deer ticks, which threatens to infect each horse with Lyme disease. They stamp their feet endlessly on the hard ground, loosening shoes, and rub themselves against anything they can find. At the moment, we are experimenting with adding two ounces of freeze-dried, finely chopped garlic to their feed, which according to its proponents is supposed to act as an insect repellent, and arrives from Canada in sealed twenty-two pound bags. But so far the bugs don't seem to have noticed, though the horses have developed a faint odor that reminds one of stepping into a French kitchen, or the Paris *Métro*.

The day begins early and busily, since Margaret is taking Dundee up to the Stoneleigh Burnham Horse Trials, in Massachusetts, leaving at 9 a.m. on the dot, which means, for Margaret, an impatient quarter to nine at the latest, with her trainer, Libby, and Juan running down the driveway to catch up with the truck, their Dunkin' Donuts breakfasts in their hands.

By seven in the morning, the other horses have been brought in from the fields, groomed, had their feet cleaned out, and fed their breakfast. Dundee, meantime, is being readied for his trip—since he won't be competing until tomorrow his mane won't be braided until he gets up there, but his tail has to be wrapped, and his legs, of course, for traveling. Some horses get worked up at all this activity—they know it means loading into the trailer, going for the trailer ride, competing—but Dundee takes it in his stride, his mind, no doubt, firmly fixed on his next meal. He is not 100 percent reliable about ditches and drops on the cross-country course yet, but one thing you can say for him, he isn't temperamental. Which is more than you can say for the rest of us.

Soon Margaret moves into her "instant departure mode." The trailer and the truck have been loaded up the day before, but there's last-minute stuff to take on board (including the horse, who is generally left to the very last), and the inevitable last-minute surprises—in this case, the keys to the trailer dressing room have gone missing, which means the door can't be locked, which in turn means that everything will need to be off-loaded on arrival at the event grounds, taken by truck to the motel, carried up to the motel rooms for the night, then back down again in the early morning.

Well, it could be worse—it could be some vital piece of tack, or perhaps worse yet one of the numerous lucky charms which Margaret carries or wears when she competes. Eventually, Dundee is brought out, looking squeaky clean, and loads into the trailer without fuss, and within seconds the whole rig is moving off down the driveway, and turning into the road. The other horses don't pay much attention. Certainly each of them, in their time, has been the one that gets loaded into the trailer, the star, but the horses, perhaps fortunately, don't seem to suffer from the kind of feelings that so afflicted Norma Desmond in *Sunset Boulevard,* and merely display a mild curiosity at Dundee's departure, then get on with the more serious business of eating.

Being a horse farm, there is no such thing as nothing to do, and Margaret's departure brings Angel out from the barn with a broom and shovel to clear shavings and manure off the driveway. Although it seems quiet, with the remaining horses in their stalls listening to music, there is, in fact, an undercurrent of constant activity. The ditch behind the washing area has to be cleaned out, not only of accumulated manure and dirt that gets hosed into it, but also because the guy who takes care of the lawn seems unable not to get grass clippings into it until it's blocked; fields need to be mowed, or dragged to break up manure; hay and straw needs to be moved down from the hayloft; shavings need to be brought in from the trailer barn where they're stored;

the feed room and the tack room need to be cleaned—ignoring the former leads to infestations of rodents, ignoring the latter simply looks sloppy—the washer and dryer have to be kept humming with dirty towels, fly masks, and pieces of horse clothing; bell boots have to be scrubbed clean and left out to dry in the sun; and then of course it's easier to pick up stalls during the day at intervals than to let it pile up to the end of the day, as is the case with so many barns.

And all this is on a day, when nothing *major* is happening, pure routine, as opposed, say, to a day when the hay man is coming, weather permitting, to deliver several tons of hay and/or straw—which means getting the hayloft rearranged and swept out to receive it, wrapping the tack room heater outlet in plastic so the propane gas stove doesn't fill up with hay and straw, and sweeping up afterward—or a day when the blacksmith is coming to shoe all the horses, or one when the vet is expected (and likely to turn up hours later than he or she was supposed to come due to an emergency along the way) to give shots or look at a horse with a problem or an injury.

None of that includes the occasional really *big* crisis or problem, of course—a sudden storm that brings a big tree down on a fence line, or a pipe finally (and without warning) giving up the ghost and cutting off the water supply to the "frost-free" hydrant in the barn (one of those plumbing repairs that looks easy at first, but—as the plumber's face grows longer and the day wears on—turns out to involve digging down three or four feet, locating the problem area, driving to the nearest plumbing supply house, fifteen miles away, and returning with a brand new hydrant, then pulling up the old one—a two-man job—installing the new one, and repacking the earth around it, a seven-hour job for which the bill will be just under a thousand dollars.

During all these crises, the horses still have to be fed, watered, groomed, taken in and out of the barn—in short, any work that has to be done, has to be done around them. They may not pay much attention, they may even be under the impression that the whole thing is being done to keep them amused, a kind of floor show, but it is absolutely necessary that their routine be disturbed as little as possible, since horses react poorly to any change in routine.

Even a "normal" day still presents ample opportunities for unexpected problems to emerge—a horse loses a shoe; a couple of bales of the hay that was just delivered yesterday and seemed fine at the time, are beginning to warm up alarmingly; there's a hornets' nest in a nearby paddock that has to be removed before it causes any problems; woodchucks, which we thought we had driven away by blocking their tunnels and holes with stones, have returned (or perhaps never really left) and are digging new holes—so there's never really a dull moment. Indeed, the calmer the horses look, the more likely it is that the people who look after them are sweating away at some intractable and unexpected task.

Anyway, with the exception of the lost trailer keys, Margaret and her crew have gone to Massachusetts, put Dundee away in temporary stabling, braided his mane, walked the cross-countr course, lugged all the tack and equipment up to their motel rooms for safekeeping, had an early dinner, gone back to do a barn check on him, and risen bright and early at 4:30 in the morning the next day to get ready for the day's competition, while back home Toby and Michael ride and "pony" the two old guys, the idea being to get all four horses exercised for the day in one go.

This isn't a bad idea. Ponying horses is dead easy, assuming your horses take to it (and most do), and the only thing you have to remember is not to wind the lead rope firmly around your hand, since there's then every chance that when the horse you're ponying stops while you're trotting on, you'll be yanked right out of the saddle (or, if you manage to keep your seat, have your arm yanked right out of its socket). Berry, as it happens, rather specializes in the odd sudden stop to admire the scenery or to drop his head and take a few mouthfuls of clover, at which point, if you're still moving forward, it feels as if you've been pulled up short by a Chieftan tank. For the most part, however, it's a slow, pleasant ride, with a slight, steady breeze that blows the bug population away and keeps the temperature down a bit. The (temporary) absence of bugs puts the horses in a good mood too—the worst thing about being a horse, one imagines, is that you present a large, unclothed, and fairly slow-moving target to biting insects of every kind, from the huge horse flies that we refer to as "B-52s" to the tiny ones with bright orange wings that sting like hell and gather in swarms, not to speak of deer flies, mosquitoes, and ticks. Apart from an occasional whiff that reminds us of Paris, the garlic does not seem to have had any effect yet. In any event, the breeze does the trick nicely, though we both know that the moment it dies down they will be out again in full force.

We're out about three-quarters of an hour—pretty much the average—and bring them back to the barn, untack them, give them each their apple. In the meantime, there's no end of things to do while the horses are inside, in addition a whole list left by Margaret of projects that need tackling.

The truth is, that with rare exceptions, the modern horse is a much under-used creature, kept idle and elaborately cared for during most of its days, and all too often only tacked up and ridden for relatively brief periods of time. For many people, in fact, *keeping* the horse has become an end in itself, a consuming and demanding occupation (or hobby) that simply overshadows in terms of time or energy the amount of riding they are ever likely to do.

The long hours spent cleaning the horse and the barn aren't a function of the animal's use (or fatigue level), but simply work performed for its own sake, and out of a deeply held notion that however run down and dirty your home may be, your barn should be spotless. Hence the number of houses of horse keepers one visits in which the tack is hanging in the bathroom, dust lies thick on every surface, muddy boots and wet ankle-length Barbour rain slickers (with their peculiarly intense smell of damp wax and horses) block the entrance, while the barn is a showplace, off the aisle of which you could eat your dinner (and might prefer to, given the state of the dining room). We don't quite fit into this category—not yet, anyway—and hope not to. In the old days, twenty years ago, when Margaret first started to compete, Roxie went with her, the two of them vanishing down our driveway in a Chevy Blazer, towing a small two-horse trailer, but nowadays Margaret tends to compete with a small *équipe*, in a new Dodge Ram truck, pulling the old gooseneck trailer with its own dressing room. Of course with a full, or nearly full barn, somebody has to stay behind and look after the horses, which also have to be exercised for the two or three days she's away. In other words, like almost everyone else, we have grown from something that was small, simple, and required one person to a much larger and more complicated undertaking, all of it, however, contained within the same old barn.

Growth, in our case, has mostly been on the outside, not the inside of the barn—more fields, more trails, more jumps and fences, while the barn itself soldiers on, now almost a quarter of a century into its latest incarnation. Every once in a while, we'll contemplate some ambitious scheme to "modernize" or "update" it, but in the end we invariably decide to leave well enough alone. It's unpretentious, unglamorous, albeit with a certain homey charm, but most of all it just *works*.

The last major job to the structure was rehanging the sliding doors at the end of the barn on new rails, since they were always getting stuck, and repainting the barn, which is something Margaret and her crew did. Otherwise, it's mostly a question of vigilant maintenance: cleaning out the gutters, touching up the paint, replacing wood that has begun to rot, and so forth.

Who knows when it was built? Perhaps as recently as seventy-five years ago—but even then it was surely built on the site of an even older barn, going back to the time of the house, which was completed in 1785—and with care it should last us through our lifetimes, and on for many more generations, until somebody buys the place who doesn't keep horses, at which point it will likely be torn down, or turned into a garage or even a pool house, God forbid. We have learned to accept its limitations without thinking too much about them, and they don't seem important anymore.

Sometimes we'll go out to the barn before dinner, just for the last look to see that everything is in good shape, and stand there for a moment drinking it in, sipping, perhaps, a glass of wine. The horses are out in their fields grazing or in their sheds, the barn is clean, empty, a gentle breeze flowing through the aisle, everything is clean, stacked in place, ready for tomorrow's use, and really it's a very good feeling, at the heart of country living for anybody who likes horses.

Way back when we first started looking at the barn and wondering if we could keep our two horses there, instead of boarding them, it didn't seem like such a big life decision, or one that would, over the years, involve so much expense, occasional heartache, and a new learning experience, not to speak of being a decision that would radically change our lives, fixing them on this house, this barn, these fields. But if we had it to do all over again, there isn't much we'd do differently. Occasionally we think that it would be nice to have more storage space, because there's never enough and maybe a couple of extra stalls, because you never know when a horse will catch your eye, or when you need some extra space for a sick horse, and so on, and so on....

Still, we've done pretty well, starting with simple beginnings, and so can anybody else who's willing to take it step by step, and to remember that step one is the desire and the determination to *do* it—the feeling, above all, that home is where your horses belong, *that it wouldn't be home without them!*

In Margaret's words: "After having our horses at home for twenty-five years, I have to admit I do sometimes wonder in the middle of the night how long will this continue. And it is a very understandable and reasonable question, as I expect many other people who keep their horses at home, and are possibly reaching a certain age, ask of themselves.

"I think sometimes, when I hear the weather forecast of upcoming blizzard conditions how nice it would be to get in some DVDs and find those books you have been looking forward to reading for so long, the old *New York Times* crossword puzzles you have been hanging on to as you have never found time to do them since your last vacation three years ago. Not spend ages dragging one layer of clothing on over another, until you are in a muck sweat and unable to move. Actually staying indoors and keeping warm, a normally unheard of thing! Instead of having to think about everything that must be set in motion before the bad weather arrives.

"What would it be like to be *happy* a snowstorm is coming instead of slightly irritated every time you hear someone say, 'Oh, it will be so beautiful' and all you can see are the exhausting problems it will create.

"How nice it would be, when I hear the rain lashing against the windows in the middle of the night, to be able to snuggle deeper into the bedclothes and enjoy the sound of it, instead of immediately worrying about whether or not the automatic waterers will overflow, or that the paddocks will be a sea of mud and should the horses be turned out they will be covered in mud from head to foot, because there's nothing like a really good roll!

"Or on a blustery windy night, with promised gusts of up to forty and fifty miles an hour, will that old tree we have been talking about getting rid of for months, finally give up the ghost and bring down some of the fence line with it?

"The winters bring out the worst in me anyway, perhaps in many other people. I wonder what happened to those wonderful African safaris and trips on houseboats along the Nile? Somehow, as the years go by, they have slipped away from us. I often wonder where the days of lazing in the garden with a book on sunny days, waving off the bugs with a fly whisk have gone, and when did I step over that imaginary line from that person to who I am now, in the barn almost as many hours as the people who work for me?

"Sometimes, when totally exhausted and exasperated over some farm-relating situation or another, we will turn to each other and say 'For God's sake let's sell this place and get a life!' Or

I will say to Michael 'I just don't know how much longer I can go on doing this.' His answer to that one is 'What else would you do?'

"Of course there are barn owners who I am sure either have to, or want to, make the decision to stop doing it. And for maybe some of the following reasons: having your horse or horses at home, with or without help, just did not turn out to be what you thought it would be. It's too much work for you on your own, or the ever more difficult problem of finding good barn help, if you do not take care of the barn yourself. Children grow up and move away and the interest just isn't there anymore. Financial reasons—and this is a big one—the costs of keeping a horse anywhere today, in a commercial boarding facility or at home, is sky-rocketing. A divorce, illness, or a death in the family. Or, of course, the fact that maybe you want a change—you just burn out.

"But in my case Michael is right, what else would I do? More important, want to do? Having been born in the country, never liked living in the big cities and wearied of traveling so much of my life, buying our property and having our horses here was 'coming home' for me. I have come full circle. It is familiar and comfortable. I can wander out after tea in the early summer evenings, pick up a treat as I go through the tack room, walk around to see each of the horses, lean over the gates, put my head against theirs. You can't beat that."

ACKNOWLEDGMENTS

With many thanks for their help to:

Rebecca Coffin

Nina Diebel, DVM

Libby Dowden

Carol Kozlowski

Tom Pavelek

Lida Tait

RESOURCES

These are some of the Web sites, magazines, and catalogs we have found useful over the years. Obviously your own list will depend on where you live, and what kind of riding you do.

Beval Saddlery
www.beval.com

Bit of Britain
www.bitofbritain.com

Dover Saddlery
www.doversaddlery.com

Dressage Extensions
www.dressageextensions.com

Equus
www.equisearch.com/magazines/equus

Everything for Horse and Rider
www.gohorses.com

Horsemen's Yankee Pedlar
www.pedlar.com

Kauffman's Saddlery
E-mail: *CharlesKauffman6@aol.com*

Rhinebeck Tack and Leather
845-876-4287

Salem Saddlery
www.salemsaddlery.com

SmartPak Equine
www.SmartPakEquine.com

Stateline Tack
www.statelinetack.com

The Horse Source (yearly)
A directory for Dutchess County and neighbors
845-724-5247

United Vet Equine
www.unitedvetequine.com

Valley Vet Supply
www.valleyvet.com

SAMPLE EXPENSE BUDGET

A record of what you have spent, and are planning to spend, on your horses can be a useful tool to help you decide where you want to put your hard-earned dollars. It can also bring you up short when you realize that you're spending the equivalent of a fabulous trip-around-the-world vacation on your passion for horses. But it's your money and having a plan can help you decide which project is the next one on your list to be financed.

You'll notice that there is no income side of the budget. That's because our assumption is that you will not be making any money from having your horses at home. The income side will come from your personal funds, or from the second mortgage you take out on your home to build the barn of your dreams, or whatever. Just be sure to include the loan payment on the expense side.

We have listed many of the expenses mentioned in the book, but you may not need some of them. Some are needed whether you have one horse, or five, and others, such as employees, may not be needed until your six-stall barn is full. That's fine—the purpose of the worksheet is to get you thinking about what you might need or want to have to keep your horses at home. And, it is also not by any means complete because everyone who keeps their horses at home has their own ideas of what is absolutely necessary and needed. Think of this as another essential barn tool.

EMPLOYEES

> Wages
> Payroll taxes
> Workmen's Comp.
> Unemployment insurance
> Housing (if applicable)
> Health-care insurance (if applicable)

BARN

> Equipment/supplies for daily upkeep
> Repairs and maintenance
> Utilities
> Property insurance
> Liability insurance
> Manure removal and maintenance of manure pile
> Loan payments (if applicable)
> Emergency fund

TURN-OUT FIELDS

> Fencing and fence maintenance
> Electric fence batteries
> Spare fence post and rails
> Mowing
> Dragging
> Seed, fertilizer, lime
> Leaf removal

FEED AND BEDDING

> Hay/alfalfa
> Straw/shavings
> Grain

Supplements
Special feeds (see pages 121–123)
"Treats"
Lime for stalls

HORSE CARE

Veterinary expenses
Equine dentist
Farrier
Horse clothing, boots, wraps, bandages
Medications
    a. Dispensed by veterinarian
    b. Medications/miscellaneous items found in catalogs, local tack shop, feed store or pharmacy
Fund for health care or injury emergency

TACK

New purchases
Repairs
Cleaning supplies

EQUIPMENT MAINTENANCE AND SERVICING

Truck and trailer
Tractor(s)
Mower(s)
Drag
4-Wheeler
Snowblower(s)
Leaf blower(s)
"Gator" or similar vehicle
Weedwhacker(s)
Fuel (diesel, gas, propane)

OUTSIDE HELP
> Trainer
> Electrician
> Plumber
> Snow removal
> Handyman
> Tree care

MISCELLANEOUS ADDITIONAL EXPENSES (If Applicable)
Maintenance of:
> Automatic waterers
> Run-in sheds
> Indoor ring
> Outdoor ring(s)

Index

Accel, 120
Acepromazine, 132
aggressive behavior, 29–30
aisles, barn, 8, 9
    cleaning, 78, 79
    fans in, 80
allergy medications, 134
anaphylactic reactions, 92
anemia, infectious, 91
Animax, 133
antibiotics, 121, 129–30, 133, 134
antihistamines, 134
anti-inflammatories, 133
antiseptics, 131
Atropine, 134
automatic watering system, 34, 76,
    78, 109, 170, 188
autumn, 171
    cleaning out paddocks in, 43–44
    daily routine in, 79
    grooming in, 89

Bacon, Richard, 7, 9–11, 23, 57, 61,
    100, 145, 156, 157
Bacon, Roxanne, 7, 9, 10, 38, 49, 56,
    57, 61–62, 75, 85, 100, 102,
    126, 146, 185
baling twine, 78
Banamine, 107, 165, 166

bandages, 153–54
Banks, Peter, 110, 111
barns, 46–47, 185–87
    boarding other people's horses
        in, 95–97
    built from scratch, 7–8
    cleaning, 10, 78, 123–26,
        180–81, 184–85
    cost of running, 47, 63, 66–67, 196
    daily routine in, 75–81
    expanding number of horses in,
        57–60
    flooding of, 39, 169
    floor plan of, 16–17
    guests in, 49–50, 55, 60
    help in, see employees
    moving horses into, 48–49
    removing snow from, 172
    renovation of, 8–11, 14–15, 57, 72
    repairs in, 110
    rules for, 56
batteries, electric fence, 43
bedding, xiv, 11, 78–80, 180
    clean and dry, 70
    cost of, 195
    purchasing, 108–9
    in run-in sheds, 34, 36
    winter stock of, 173
bell boots, 152–53

Berry, 101, 163, 164, 183
bit guards, 145
bits, 144
    cleaning, 146
blacksmiths, *see* farriers
blankets, 76, 149–51
    damage to, 29
    for older horses, 166
    racks for, 10, 18
    turn-out, 78
Blinkhorn, Nancy, 74, 144
Blinkhorn, Tamzin, 62, 74
blood tests, 91
    for Lyme disease, 92–93
Blue Seal feeds, 119
boarding, xiv, 46, 48, 54, 63
    medical certificates required
        for, 91
    of other people's horses, 95–97
boots
    bell, 152–53
    galloping, 86, 153
Boucher bits, 144
Boyce, Toby, 102, 109, 110, 165, 183
Boyer, Katherine, 48
bran mash, 121
breastplates, 145
breeding horses, 64
bridles, 86, 142–43
    brackets for, 11
    taking off, 84
brood mares, 117
brushes, 10, 18
buckets
    cleaning, 171
    feed, 118
    water, *see* water buckets
bush-hogging, 58, 59, 159

Cady, Matt, 109
carts, 160
cavessons, 144
cleaning, 123–26
    of barn, 10, 78, 123–26, 180–81,
        184–85
    equipment for, 10, 125, 126
    of horse clothing, 152
    routine for, 78
    of run-in sheds, 34, 78
    of tack, 80, 145–47
clipping, 89–90
clothing, horse, 78, 149–54
cobwebs, removing, 79
Coffin, Rebecca, 111
Coggins Test, 91
colic, 3, 95, 121, 164–65
competitions, 5, 6, 177–79, 182–83,
    185
    barn routine and, 76, 77
    employees and, 102
    horses ridden in, 6, 51, 57, 58, 118
    medical certificates required
        for, 91
    older horses in, 163
    tack for, 142–45
coolers, 87, 151
corn oil, 120, 165
costs, *see* expenses
cowboys, 28
cross-country trials, 65–66, 86, 102,
    111, 144, 153, 158, 177, 179,
    182–83
crusades, 167
Cruz, Delores, 110
Cruz, Juan, 102, 109, 110, 179
curb chains, 146
Cushing's disease, 166

dairy farms, 22
conversion to horse farms
of, 26
deer hunters, 37–38
Deffand, Marquis de, 57
Denis, St., 57
dental care, 90–91, 166
Desitin, 85
Dexamethazone, 134
Diebel, Nina, 110
Diphenhydramine, 134
Dowden, Libby, 100, 111, 179
Doxycycline Hyclate, 133
drags, 161
drainage systems, 25
dressage, 86, 89
tack for, 141–43
drought, 31, 39
Dumpsters, 74
Dundee, 93, 106, 178–80, 183

Egyptians, ancient, 69
electric fencing, 27, 37
replacing batteries for, 43
electrical wiring, 10, 14
electrolytes, 120, 130, 166
emergencies, 77, 102
vet fees for, 103–4
employees, 62, 87, 99–102
boarded horses and, 95
cost of, 196
daily routine and, 75
horses belonging to, 97
rules and, 56–57
veterinarians and, 104, 105
in winter, 173
Encephalitis, 92
equine infectious anemia, 91

Equine Protozoal Myeloen-
cephalitis (EPM), 93
equipment, 155–62, 197
event riding, *see* competitions
Excalibur sheath cleaner, 90
expenses, 47, 63, 66–67, 194–97
barn, 196
bedding, 195
boots, 152–53
buildings and improvements,
196–97
employee, 196
equipment, 197
feed, 195
grounds, 197
horse clothing, 150
shoeing, 107–8
tack, 143–44, 195–96
veterinary care, 63, 67, 103–4, 195
eye ointments, 134

fall, *see* autumn
fans, 80, 118, 124
farms, 21–22
condition of land on, 22–25
horse, 2–3, 63
replaced by development, 46
farriers, xiv, 63, 105–8, 112–15, 173
older horses and, 107, 164, 166
feed and feeding, xiv, 11, 63,
117–21, 179
aggressive horses and, 29–30
contamination of, 93
cost of, 195
for older horses, 118, 119, 165–66
purchasing, 108–9
routine for, 78–80, 84
winter stock of, 173

feed buckets, 11, 15
feed room, 9, 18, 19, 126
   cleaning, 80, 181
   renovation of, 10
feed tubs, 10, 30
   in run-in sheds, 36
feet, grooming, 84, 85
fencing, 22, 25–27, 38, 63, 185
   gates in, 29
   maintaining, 27–28, 30, 42, 110, 158, 162
   "Secretariat," 30, 60
   security of, 28–29
fields, 39, 102, 185
   clearing, 58–59
   fencing, 28, 37
   liming, 43
   manure spread on, 71, 73, 74
   mowing, 42, 65
   turning horses out into, 29, 37–38
fire alarms, 14, 124
fire extinguishers, 124
fleeces, synthetic, 145
flies, 80, 118, 119, 170, 178, 183
flooding, 39, 77, 169, 170–71
Flunixin Meglumine, 133
Flu vaccine, 92
fly masks, 151
foals, 117
forklifts, 159
four-wheelers, 157, 160, 174

galloping boots, 86, 153
garage, 19, 109
   laundry facilities in, 20
garlic, 120, 178, 184
gates, 29

Gators, 157, 160, 174
girths, 142
grain, 30, 78
Grand Complete, 120
grass, 79, 80, 122–23, 171
   planting, 30–31, 38
   see also mowing
grooming, xiv, 55, 83–90, 155, 179
   equipment for, 10, 18
   routine for, 78–80
guests
   barn tours for, 49–50, 60
   discouraging riding by, 51–55

hacking, 86
halters, 10, 30, 84, 174
handymen, 109–10
hay, 30, 63, 65, 78, 121–22, 181
   for older horses, 165–66
   morning, 78
   purchasing, 79, 108–9, 122
   in run-in sheds, 36
hay loft, 9
   cleaning, 79
   lights in, 14
health problems, 2–3, 20
   see also veterinarians; *specific ailments*
heating devices, 34, 36, 173
hedge trimmers, 161
help, *see* employees
hoof ailments, 60
hoof dressings, 136
hoof picks, 10, 14, 69, 84
Hoof Toughner, 85
horse clothing, 78, 149–54
hoses, 14
house guests, *see* guests

hunting season, 37–38
hunt trails, 46, 48, 49, 158
hustle, 30

Ichthammol, 85
income-producing activities, 64–66
indoor riding ring, xiv, 39, 63, 174
injuries, 37, 53, 67
  checking for, 85–86
  from hunters, 38
  treatment of, 130, 131
  from turning out horses
    together, 29
insect repellents, 136
  garlic as, 120, 178, 184
insecticides, 124
insects, 171, 178, 183–84
  see also flies; ticks
insurance, 52, 99, 197
interval training, 86
Ivermectrin, 94
Irish knits, 151
irrigation, 31
Isoxsuprine, 134

Jessup, Tim, 106
jumps, 31, 65, 86, 97, 101, 153, 163,
    177, 185
Juress, Detleff, 19, 34, 109

KK bits, 144
Kozlowski, Carol, 89

laminitis, 122, 134n
laundry facilities, 19, 109, 181
  cleaning, 80
lawsuits, 52–53, 96
lead ropes, 10

leaf blowers, 160
leaves, fallen, 43–44
Lexol, 146
liability insurance, 99
lighting, 14
liming
  of fields, 43
  of stall floors, 78, 80
Lonesome Dove (McMurtry), 28
lunge lines, 145
Lyme disease, 43, 92–93, 133, 178

machinery, 155–62, 173
mane, grooming, 84, 87, 89
manure pile, 29, 39, 71–75, 172
  burning, 74
  hauling out, 110
  location of, 72
  raking area around, 80–81
  in winter, 174
martingales, 144
McDonald, Eddie, 26, 30
McMurtry, Larry, 28
mechanical equipment, 155–62
medications, 11, 119, 126–28
  basic lists of, 128–35
  see also specific drugs
Miguel, Angel, 102, 109, 110, 180
Missouri, 30, 89, 107, 121, 163–65
Monday Morning Disease, 2
mosquitoes, 171, 183
mounting block, 87, 88
mowing, 42, 157–60, 162, 180
muck bucket, 11
mucking stalls, xiv, 78, 80, 155
mud, xiv, 25, 39, 171, 188
  cleaning off, 85
Murphy, Mike, 38

nameplates, 10, 18
 cleaning, 146
Nathe bits, 144
Native Americans, 68–69
navicular disease, 134
Neatsfoot oil, 147
Nebraska, 163
Never Dull, 146
notice boards, 138–39
Nutrena feeds, 119

older horses, 30, 67, 163–68, 171,
 183
 feed for, 118, 119, 165–66
 medications for, 134
 shoeing, 107, 164, 166
 supplements for, 121, 165
 veterinarians and, 105–6,
 165–67
outbuildings, 19, 109–10
outdoor riding ring, 31

paddocks, 22, 28–44, 102, 158
 boarded horses in, 95–96
 clearing out, 43–44
 fencing of, *see* fencing
 during hunting season, 37–38
 manure pile next to, 73
 maps of, 32–33, 40–41
 mowing, 42
 preparing land for, 30–31
 rotating, 79
 run-in sheds in, 34–37
 turning horses out in, 29
 water sources in, 11, 31–32, 34,
 43, 76, 78, 109
 wet, 85, 171, 188
 in winter, 61, 174

pain medications, 133
Panacur Powerpac, 94
pasture, 29
 turning farmland into, 22–25,
 31, 38
 see also fields; paddocks
Pavelek, Tom, 106
Pelham bits, 144
penicillin, 133
Pepto Bismol, 130
Phenylbutazone, 133
pigs, 30
pitch forks, 11
Plains Indians, 69
PolyPads, 147
ponying, 87–88, 97, 164, 183
post and rail fencing, 26, 27, 30
posted land, 37
Potomac Horse Fever (PHF), 92
probiotics, 121, 129–30
pumps, submersible, 39, 169

quarter sheets, 151

rabies shots, 91
rain, torrential, 77, 169–71
rainsheets, 150–51, 169
rakes, 11
reins, 143–45
 cleaning, 146
residential development, 46
Rhinebeck Equine, 103
Rhinebeck Tack Shop, 141
Rhino vaccine, 92
riding schedule, 78, 86
rings, 58
 indoor, xiv, 39, 63, 174
 outdoor, 31

Roe, Harold, 7, 25, 37, 58–59, 73, 109, 157–58
rubbing alcohol, 129
run-in sheds, 34–37, 76, 109
    cleaning of, 34, 78, 79, 81, 160
    in winter, 174
Rutledge, Norm, 106

saddle pads, 147
saddles, 86, 141–42
    cleaning, 11, 55, 145–46
    rack for, 11, 145
salt blocks, 11, 36, 120
Scythians, ancient, 68
"Secretariat" fencing, 30, 60
shampooing, 84, 135
shavings, *see* bedding
sheaths, cleaning, 90
shedding blades, 14, 87
sheds, *see* run-in sheds
sheep, 21, 22
sheep wire, 9, 14
shipping wraps and bandages, 153–54
shoes
    checking, 84, 169
    see also farriers
shots, xiv, 91–93, 132, 135
    for older horses, 164
shovels, 11
shows, *see* competition
ShowSheen, 84, 135–36
Slezak, Len, 110
smoke detectors, 14
snap test, 93
snow, riding in, 171–72
snowblowers, 161, 173
snowplowing, 109–10, 173–74
Spanish *conquistadores*, 167

splint boots, 153
sponges, 14, 145
spring, 171
    barn routine in, 79
    grass in, 123
    grooming in, 87, 89
stable, *see* barn
stable sheets, 78, 84
stadium jumps, 31, 86, 102, 144
stalls, 8, 14–15, 57
    fans in, 80
    floor plan of, 14
    mucking, xiv, 78, 80, 155
    older horses in, 166–67
    renovating, 9, 10
    routine for cleaning, 78, 79
standing wraps, 154
steroids, 133
stirrup leathers, 142
stirrups, 142
    cleaning, 146
Stoneleigh Burnham Horse Trials, 178–79
storms, severe, 77, 172–75
strangles vaccine, 91
straw, *see* bedding
Strongid, 94, 165
Stübbens saddles, 141–42
studs, 86
submersible pumps, 39
Sulfamethoxazole, 133
summer, 170–71, 178
    barn routine in, 76 77, 79–80
    feed in, 118, 119
    horse care in, 85, 90
    run-in sheds in, 34, 35
    tack care in, 147
    vet calls in, 105

supplements, 117–20
  for older horses, 121, 165
surcingles, 145
sweat scrapers, 14

Tabasco, 54, 57, 62
tack, 141–48, 178
  cleaning, 80, 145–47
  cost of, 143–44, 195–96
tack room, 8, 10, 20
  cleaning, 80, 181
  fire alarm in, 14
  medicine cabinet in, 126
  renovation of, 9, 11
  supplies in, 135–28
tail, grooming, 84, 89
teeth, care of, 90–91, 166
temperature taking, 86
Tetanus, 92
Thoroughbreds, 26, 54, 143
thrush, 70, 85, 136, 169
ticks, 43, 85, 120, 171, 178, 183
towels, 78–79, 128
tractors, 42, 58–59, 156–60, 162
trailers, 58, 185
  barn for, 109
  boarding and, 96
  loading, 88, 179
trails, xiv, 39, 42, 46, 48, 49, 58,
    102, 185
  clearing, 58, 59, 110, 158
training, xiv
  of competition horses, 6, 58
  routine for, 86
  undoing, by inexperienced
    riders, 53
tranquilizers, 132

traveling, care for horses during,
    47–48, 76
treats, 139–40, 166
trees, 43–44, 110
Trimethoprim, 133
turning-out, xiv, 78, 122
  areas for, 39 (*see also* fields;
    paddocks)
  blankets for, 149, 150
  of boarded horses, 95

urination, 85, 87, 166

vaccines, 91–93
vacuuming, 85
veterinarians, xiv, 38, 86, 102–5,
    111–12, 115
  bills of, 63, 67, 103–4, 195
  cleaning sheaths by, 90
  in emergencies, 77
  injections administered by, 91–93
  medications obtained from,
    132–35
  older horses and, 105–6, 165–67
  treats given to horses by, 139

water buckets, 11, 15, 31
  filling, 79
  in run-in sheds, 36
  scrubbing, 78, 80
watering system, automatic, 34, 76,
    78, 109, 170, 188
water jumps, 107, 153, 177
water tubs, 11, 31–32, 36
  contamination of, 93
  in winter, 32, 34
Watnick, Jay, 63–65

Watnick, Marianna, 63, 64
weather, 169–71
    severe, 77, 172–75
        see also summer; winter
weedwacking, 158, 161
Weissbecker, Mark, 145
West Nile virus, 92
wheelbarrows, 11
winter, xiv, 61, 67, 169–75, 187–88
    barn routine in, 76, 77, 80
    horse care in, 85, 89, 90
    horse clothing for, 151
    manure pile in, 73
    older horses in, 166, 167

run-in sheds in, 34–36
shoeing in, 107
vet calls in, 105
water troughs in, 31, 34, 43
wire fencing, 30, 37
woods, second growth, 22
Worker's Compensation, 99
worming, xiv, 91, 93–94, 135
    of older horses, 164, 165
wounds, medications for, 130, 131
woven wire fencing, 30
wraps, 153–54

Yontef, Stuart, 66

BOOKS BY MICHAEL KORDA

COUNTRY MATTERS
The Pleasures and Tribulations of Moving from a
Big City to an Old Country Farmhouse

ISBN 0-06-095748-4 (paperback)
With his inimitable sense of humor and storytelling
talent, *New York Times* bestselling author Michael
Korda brings us this charming, hilarious, self-
deprecating memoir of a city couple's new life in
the country. Sure to have readers in stitches, this is
a book that appeals to all who have ever dreamed
of owning that perfect little place in the country.

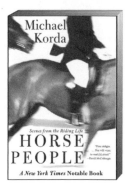

HORSE PEOPLE
Scenes from the Riding Life

ISBN 0-06-093676-2 (paperback)
An entertaining and intimate view of the people
and animals that populate the horse world—from
farmers and work horses, to policemen and their
mounts, wealthy investors and their racing
thoroughbreds, cowboys and wild horses, and
little girls and their ponies.

CHARMED LIVES
A Family Romance

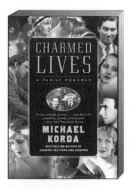

ISBN 0-06-008556-8 (paperback)
Rising from obscurity in the Hungarian
countryside to the pinnacle of Hollywood society,
Sir Alexander Korda was the embodiment of the
Cinderella legend—but his darker impulses nearly
brought his family to its knees. His brothers,
Zoltan and Vincent, led similarly charmed lives
in circles that included H. G. Wells, Winston
Churchill, and Alex's wife Merle Oberon. With a
loving but undeceived eye, Michael Korda
recounts their trials and successes.
